J. D. O'Connor
Clare Fletcher

SOUNDS ENGLISH

A PRONUNCIATION PRACTICE BOOK

Consultant: Joanne Kenworthy

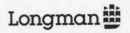
Longman

Longman Group UK Limited,
Longman House, Burnt Mill, Harlow,
Essex CM20 2JE, England
and Associated Companies throughout the world.

First published 1989

Illustrated by Chris Burke, Susannah English, Diane Fisher, Hardlines,
           Helen Manning, Pat Moffat, Stephen Wright

Set in 10/11 pt Century Light.

Produced by Longman Singapore Publishers Pte Ltd.
Printed in Singapore.

ISBN 0 582 01439 5

Contents

Introduction for independent students

If you are working on your own to improve your English pronunciation, this introduction and the Introductory Unit on pages 22–27 are especially for you. Study these first, to help you make the best use of this book and cassette.

IMPROVING YOUR ENGLISH PRONUNCIATION

This book provides practice in hearing and saying the sounds of English. If you want to have a good pronunciation of English, you need to be able to make all the *sound contrasts* used in English. You must be able to distinguish 'light' from 'right', 'fit' from 'feet', 'right' from 'ride', etc, both in listening and speaking. The number of contrasts is different in different languages; some English sounds will be similar to those in your language, but some will be different.

The first thing you must do is to decide which of the English contrasts are difficult for you and which are easy. If you already know this, use the *Sound list* on page 14. This has a list of all the English sounds, each one with a phonetic symbol and a key word. (Don't be afraid of the phonetic symbols; they are used because some different sounds have the same spelling, e.g. 'thin' and 'this' begin with different sounds but have the same 'th' spelling, so we use the phonetic symbols /θ/ and /ð/ to show that there is a difference.) Against each sound you will find the number of all the units in which it is practised. If you know, for example, that the /θ/ sound in 'thin' is difficult for you, you can easily find the pages which will help you.

If you are not sure which English contrasts you need to practise, look at the *Language chart* on pages 15–17. This will tell you, for various languages, which contrasts are difficult, and the *units* and *tasks* in the book which will help with these contrasts.

By using the Sound list and Language chart, plan a pronunciation programme for yourself. You should study the Introductory Unit first because it shows you how the other units are organised. After that, begin with any of the units you have chosen for your programme.

OUTLINE OF THE UNITS

Units based on a sound contrast

Units 1–18, 23–31

Each unit takes two, three or four English sounds. It begins with listening practice. This is most important, because if you cannot hear the difference between the sounds, you will never be able to make the difference. When we learn our own language as babies, we learn to recognise certain sounds as important, and to say those sounds. It is as if we develop a box in our brain for each sound. When we hear a sound, we put it in the correct box, and understand it. When we speak, we take the right sounds out of their boxes. But different languages have different sets of sounds: they need different boxes. And you need to listen carefully and repeatedly to English sounds to develop the right sound 'boxes' for English. After listening, you must practise saying the words containing the sounds.

The unit then provides practice of each sound in context, in a short passage, conversation or reading text, followed by similar practice containing two (or sometimes three or four) sounds. The conversations and texts are all recorded, so you can listen to English speakers before you practise yourself.

Many of the texts are followed by exercises. Learners of English often find that they can say a difficult sound correctly when they are thinking about *how* to say it, but when they have to think about grammar and vocabulary and the meaning of what they want to say, they go back to the old incorrect way. The exercises help to overcome this problem. You have to answer questions, or make your own conversations, thinking about *what* to say, as well as *how* to say it.

Other units

Units 19, 20, 22 and 32
These units are slightly different; in them you do not begin by listening to pairs of words containing the sounds. Instead, you meet the sounds in context straight away.

Unit 21
This unit practises linking words together smoothly.

Spelling

Units 1–6 and 23–32 contain a Spelling box. English spelling is not always a good guide to pronunciation. There are often different ways to write a sound. The Spelling box shows you the common and less common ways of spelling each sound in that unit and looks like this:

SPELLING

/eə/ there

Common:
ALL   **air** chair
MANY **are** care
         ary Mary

Less common:
ear pear

Exceptions:
ere where
         there
eir their

Common ways of spelling the sound /eə/.

ALL means that all words with this spelling are pronounced with this sound.

MANY means that many words with this spelling are pronounced with this sound, but some are not. (Other headings are MOST and SOME.) The headings help you work out the likely pronunciation of a new word.

Exceptions – useful words with unusual spellings.

Stress and intonation

As well as the *sounds* of English, the stress and intonation are important. Some words and syllables are pronounced more strongly than others: they are *stressed*. The voice rises and falls as we speak, and the tune of the voice helps to show what we mean: this is 'intonation'. Each unit contains some stress or intonation practice: in that part of the unit, *stressed* syllables are shown in **bold** type.

On pages 18–21 there is a list of the intonation patterns practised in the book. This gives a brief explanation of each one, and a list of the *units* and *tasks* in the book in which they are to be found. So if you want, for example, to practise question tags, you can easily find all the tasks in which they occur.

Timing of pronunciation work

The best way to work on pronunciation is 'little and often'. It is better to spend fifteen minutes every day than two hours once a week. It is not necessary to practise one whole unit at a time. Each unit is made up of several tasks and you can do one or two tasks at a time. A whole unit will take about one hour.

How to make the sounds of English

This is a practice book, and does not tell you how the sounds are made. If you want to find out more about how to pronounce English, read *Better English Pronunciation* by J D O'Connor.

Introduction for teachers

This book aims to help students to improve their pronunciation of English. It is based on four principles.

1 The importance of contrasts

Every language is composed of a limited number of sounds which a native speaker can distinguish without difficulty. But languages differ in the number and nature of these sounds. If a contrast between two sounds does not exist in one's own language, it can be difficult to distinguish between them in another language. The Japanese beginner, for example does not have the contrast which makes the difference /l, r/ or /b, v/ so obvious for a native English speaker. Consequently 'I love you' may become 'I rub you'.

2 The importance of listening

The key to the development of the essential contrasts is concentrated listening. A baby who is born deaf cannot hear the speech of others and may, in the worst case, remain completely mute. Similarly, students who cannot hear a particular English contrast have no chance of reproducing it. Until Japanese students can *hear* the contrast between 'light' and 'right', or Spanish students between 'boat' and 'vote', they have no chance of *making* the difference.

This book provides listening material to help students master contrasts that are difficult for them. Students must be encouraged to listen carefully, and to listen a good deal. Time spent on listening is *never* wasted.

3 The importance of concentrated practice

New speech habits require a great deal of practice. The performance of a new contrast, once it can be heard, involves a new orientation of the motor control centre in the brain to produce unfamiliar muscular movements. The first stage must be to concentrate on minimally different pairs of words exhibiting the contrast, so that the student is not distracted by other difficulties. At this stage, any contrast which the student can produce, and which an English speaker can recognise, is adequate. The sounds may not be exactly what a native speaker would produce, but fine tuning of the actual sounds can be done gradually.

It is not enough for the students to produce the contrast satisfactorily once or twice or three times. They must be brought to the point where, at any rate in classroom conditions, they can do it every time, so that, for example, French speakers *always* say 'air' when they mean 'air', and 'hair' when they mean 'hair', and not vice versa. This calls for diligent practice.

4 The importance of the transition from controlled practice to free speech

It is a familiar situation that students can produce a sound correctly in a class, when they are concentrating on it exclusively, but revert to their previous, faulty, pronunciation at other times when they have to cope with grammar and vocabulary and the general shaping of what they want to say. Each unit therefore provides gradually freer exercises, still with many examples of the relevant sounds, where students have to maintain their production gains in face of other demands.

PLANNING A PRONUNCIATION PROGRAMME

The sounds which will be difficult for your students are those which are not present in their own language. Speakers of Spanish, for example, will have different needs from speakers of Japanese. After Unit 1, you can start work on *any* unit, and there are two features of the book which will help you to select the units most useful for your students.

1 Sound list

On page 14 is a list of all the sounds of English, with a complete schedule of all the units in which each sound is practised. If you know that your students need practice in, e.g., /θ, ð/, this list will show you all the units where these sounds can be found. English spelling is notoriously difficult for foreign learners: e.g. 'thin' and 'then' have different initial sounds but no difference in the spelling, so we have provided a phonetic symbol plus a key word for each sound. Use of the book does not depend on the student, or teacher, knowing the phonetic symbols, and how far you make use of them in your lessons is entirely up to you. (Students who are familiar with the phonetic alphabet will be able to look up the pronunciation of words in the current editions of all the major ELT dictionaries, which use the same symbols as this book.)

2 Language chart

The table on pages 15–17 shows which *units* and *tasks* are most useful for a number of different languages. This will help you to concentrate on the relevant units. In some cases not all the tasks in a particular unit are necessary, e.g. in German and Cantonese, / t, d / are difficult only in final position in the word, so we have indicated which tasks are relevant.

By using these lists you can plan a pronunciation programme for your particular students.

This is a *practice* book, and does not explain how to make the sounds. You will find a clear description of how the sounds are made, and advice for producing them, in *Better English Pronunciation* by J D O'Connor.

Stress and intonation

The arrangement of the book is based on the *sounds* of English. However, within each unit there is also some practice of an aspect of stress or intonation which appears in the material of the unit. Stress and intonation are thus practised in context.

A list of the intonation patterns used is given on pages 18–21, together with the *units* and *tasks* in which they are to be found. So if you want, for example, to practise question tags, you can easily find all the tasks in which they occur.

Timing of pronunciation work

The best way to work on pronunciation is 'little and often'. Each unit is made up of several self-contained tasks. Ten or fifteen minutes could be spent at the beginning or end of each lesson, working on one task each time. A whole unit will take about one hour.

Which English pronunciation?

The cassettes which accompany this book use what is often referred to as Received Pronunciation (RP for short) – the pronunciation of educated native speakers in the south-east of England. Which form of English pronunciation students use will depend on where they are. In an area where a variety of English is spoken with a different accent, that would normally be the model students would acquire. In some English accents, for example, including most American accents, /r/ is pronounced in words like 'bird', and students would use that form in their own speech. In any case, students can be reassured that accents of English have far more similarities than differences.

OUTLINE OF THE UNITS
Unit 1 – Introductory Unit

The Introductory Unit consists of a typical unit, with a commentary explaining the exercises and giving suggestions for using them. This is especially necessary for students working alone, but you might also find it useful to work through it with a class. The sound contrast involved is /ɪ, e/, and students needing to work on that contrast should certainly work on this unit.

Units based on a sound contrast
Units containing two sounds

Each unit begins with listening practice to help students learn to hear the difference between two sounds. (This includes the contrast between 'h' and 'no-h', as in 'heat' and 'eat'.) Also at this stage (Task 1), students practise producing the sounds in individual words. The unit then provides practice of each sound in context, followed by material containing both sounds in context. The students' production moves from repetition and drilling, to freer speech in which the student has to decide what to say, within a framework which ensures a plentiful occurrence of the sounds being practised.

Units containing three sounds

These follow a similar progression to two-sound units. Any individual speaker will usually need to concentrate on two of the three sounds. In Unit 14 /b, v, w/ for example, Spanish speakers will concentrate on the difference between /b/ and /v/ (Tasks 1, 2, 4 and 5), while German and Indian students will concentrate on /v/ and /w/ (Tasks 1, 3, 4 and 5). Combining three sounds in this way provides more practice material for more people in the space available.

Units containing four sounds

The three units dealing with 'th' each contain four sounds. The pair of voiceless and voiced sounds /θ/ and /ð/ are contrasted in turn with /s, z/ (Unit 16), /t, d/ (Unit 17), and /f, v/ (Unit 18).

Other units

Unit 32 /aɪ, ɔɪ, aʊ/
These diphthongs are included for completeness. Distinguishing them is not a
problem for most learners. There is therefore no task contrasting the sounds.
Instead the unit concentrates on using them in context.

Unit 22 a(gain)
This unit provides practice in perceiving and producing the sound /ə/ in
unstressed syllables and weak forms of words.

Units 19 and 20 Consonant clusters
These units provide practice in producing various clusters of consonants, at
the beginning of words in Unit 19, and in the middle and at the end of words in
Unit 20.

Unit 21 Linking of words
This unit practises the smooth linking of words beginning with a vowel to the
preceding word.

HOW TO USE THE MATERIAL

Focussing on contrasting sounds

In Units 1–18 and 23–31, the first task is to distinguish between the contrasted
sounds. In 1.1, students listen to minimal pairs – pairs of words which are
identical* except for the sounds contrasted: e.g. 'see/she', 'sell/shell'.

In 1.2, they hear one word from a pair, and have to identify which word it is. If
students cannot do this at first, leave it until they have had further listening
practice. The correct words are given in the Key.

1.3 contains minimal pairs in the context of a sentence.

In 1.2 and 1.3, the instructions in the book tell students to write down the word
they hear. In a class, you might instead ask students to *show* which sound they
hear, so that you can see at once how they are doing. They can do this by putting
up their left hand for sound 1 and their right hand for sound 2, or, with two cards
of different colours, holding up one colour for sound 1 and the other for sound 2.

Further practice in identifying sounds can be given in two ways. Of course, you
can play tasks 1.2 and 1.3 several times, but after a time the order of words
becomes familiar, and the listener can remember which word comes next, without
recognising the sound. To get round this, wind the tape on a little way, and play a
word or sentence at random. Wind back and forward to pick out words in a

---

*   All the pairs in the book are minimal pairs in RP. In a few cases, some accents of English pronounce
    other sounds in the word differently, e.g. in accents which pronounce /r/ wherever it occurs, pairs
    such as 'stock/stalk', 'not/nought' are minimal pairs, but 'pot/port' is not, since as well as a different
    vowel quality, the second word has an /r/ sound. If such an accent is prevalent where you are
    teaching, skip over the pairs that don't work, and concentrate on the majority that do.

different order. Thus, you might play d) a) f) h) b) e) g). You can still use the key to check the word on the tape. In this way, you can practise as often as needed.

Alternatively, a teacher can say words or sentences for a class.

The words and sentences in Task 1 should also be used for practice in saying the two sounds. Students can repeat them after the voice on tape, or read them from the book. Then a student can say a word or sentence which the teacher and the rest of the class must identify. Make sure students understand that the sentences in the book, e.g.

I'm waiting for the bill/bell.

represent two separate sentences:

I'm waiting for the bill.
I'm waiting for the bell.

The vocabulary in the minimal pairs may occasionally include an unfamiliar word. For pronunciation purposes, it doesn't matter if the word is not known. However, students naturally want to understand what they are hearing and saying. Use your discretion as to how often and when to explain vocabulary.

Presentation and practice of texts/conversations

Stage 1: Three methods are suggested, which can be used to vary the approach.
Method A: Play the complete text/conversation; students listen, with books open or closed.
Method B: Play the text/conversation; students listen and underline* the words containing the sound being practised. Stop the tape as necessary to give students time to do this. For texts/conversations with more than one sound, you can play the tape more than once, or concentrate on one sound in the first half, and the other in the second.
Method C: Ask students to look at the text/conversation and underline* the words containing the sound. (This is easier for sounds with regular spelling e.g. /p, b/; for others, use Method A or B instead).

Stage 2: Students listen and repeat, phrase by phrase. (With longer conversations, you may want to limit this repetition to part of the conversation. Occasionally, you may want to skip this stage altogether.)

Stage 3: Students practise the text/conversation. Divide students into pairs to practise conversations. For continuous texts, too, students can usefully work with a partner, listening and helping each other. While the class is working, the teacher can go round listening and helping students, and noticing which students have mastered the sounds and which need further work.

Exploitation of the text/conversation

Many of the texts are followed by exercises. Here, the students move beyond reproducing a text/conversation from the book. They have to answer questions, or make their own conversations, or discuss with others. So they have to think what

---

* If students are working from class textbooks, they should write the words in their own notebooks. Also, where there are charts or texts to be completed, students should first copy them into their own notebooks.

to say – but still make the sounds correctly. Some of the exercises require students to work together:

(GW) *Example from Unit 3*

4.1   **How much do you enjoy the things in the chart below –**
1 very much?   2 not much?   3 not at all?
Fill in the chart for yourself, then ask three other people.

	You			
playing chess watching TV washing up going to a football match cooking chips eating chips lying in the sunshine shopping				

Now tell the rest of the class what you found.

e.g. Maria doesn't like watching TV much. Jean and David like watching TV, but they don't like washing up.

In the final stage, a few students can report to the whole class, or students can report their findings to a group within the class – which would give more people a chance to speak.

Some exercises ask students to make a number of conversations following a model in the book, with slightly different content each time. It may be helpful to get students to underline in the printed conversation the parts to be changed each time. Alternatively the teacher can write up the framework on the board. Encourage partners to exchange roles in the second and subsequent versions. (Exercises marked with the symbol ** have one side of the conversation recorded on the cassette; this is primarily intended for independent students rather than class use.)

The symbols **(PW)** and **(GW)** indicate pairwork and groupwork.

Some exercises involve tasks which *can* be done by an individual, e.g.

Below are some events from a story. With a partner, decide the right order. Tell the story.

It would be possible for individuals in silence to number the events in the likely order. However, since the aim is to practise pronunciation, students should be encouraged to talk about it. Here too, it is useful for students to work with a partner or in a small group. There should be a busy hum in the classroom.

The teacher's role at this point in the lesson is to arrange the students into pairs or groups, and to monitor their work. Students will be concentrating on what they are saying; if necessary, remind them *how* to say it – or make a note of points to practise afterwards.

Spelling

All the vowel units and some of the consonant units (Units 2–6) have a Spelling box. Consonant sounds whose spelling is fairly straightforward do not have a Spelling box. The Spelling box shows the main ways in which a particular sound can be spelt.

S P E L L I N G

/eə/ there

Common:
ALL **air** chair
MANY **are** care
     ary Mary

Less common:
ear pear

Exceptions:
ere where
     there
eir their

The heading *Common* means that this is a common way of spelling that sound. Some commonly occurring words have unusual spellings, e.g. 'people'. Such words are included as *Exceptions*. Unusual words with unusual spellings are omitted.

ALL means that all words with this spelling are pronounced with this sound. MANY means that many words with this spelling are pronounced with this sound, but some are not. Other headings are MOST and SOME. This helps students work out the likelihood of a particular pronunciation for a new word which they have read. (There are useful rules for working out pronunciation from spelling in *Teaching English Pronunciation* by Joanne Kenworthy, Chapter 5.4.)

Individual sounds

/l/ Work on /l/ in Units 11, 12 and 19 concentrates on /l/ before vowels, e.g. 'light', 'follow', 'play'. A recognisable /l/ sound is essential here for intelligibility.
  There is no specific work on words such as 'ball', where the / l / is at the end of the word, or 'salt', where it precedes a consonant. The correct formation of /l/ here is less crucial. If students produce a vowel-like sound similar to /ʊ/, this is intelligible (and indeed is being used by an increasing number of English speakers). For most students who have difficulty with /l/, there are more pressing pronunciation needs than work on final /l/.

/r/ Units 11, 12 and 19 concentrate on /r/ before vowels, e.g. 'red', 'marry', 'fresh' – positions in which it is pronounced in all accents of English. In RP, it is not pronounced before consonants, or at the end of a word, e.g. 'bird', 'car'. Some accents of English do pronounce /r/ in these positions (most American accents do). It is therefore not a high priority to *stop* students saying /r/ in these positions; if they pronounce /r/ in words like 'bird' and 'car' it will not hinder intelligibility. However, it may contribute to a marked foreign accent, particularly if the /r/ is strongly retroflex or rolled. So, some students may need practice in *not* saying /r/ in words like 'bird' and 'car'. Units 29 and 31 contain plenty of suitable material.

/m/ Unit 15. Students do not usually have difficulty distinguishing /m/ from other sounds, so there is no listening practice for /m/. But some students do have difficulty saying /m/ , especially at the ends of words, so there is a task on this (Task 2).

References

Better English Pronunciation by J D O'Connor, Cambridge University Press
Teaching English Pronunciation by Joanne Kenworthy, Longman

Sound list

This list gives the sounds of English, with a key word to illustrate each sound. It shows the units in the book in which each sound is practised.

Sound	Key word	Units in which the sound is practised	Sound	Key word	Units in which the sound is practised
s	so	2, 6, 16	ə	again	22
z	zoo	6, 16	i:	see	23
ʃ	shop	2, 3	ɪ	if	1, 23
ʒ	pleasure	4	e	egg	1, 24, 30
tʃ	chin	3, 4	æ	hand	24, 25
dʒ	judge	4, 5	ʌ	up	25
f	five	13, 18	ɒ	hot	26
v	voice	13, 14, 18	ɔ:	saw	26, 27
θ	thin	16, 17, 18	əʊ	home	27
ð	this	16, 17, 18	u:	food	28
p	pen	8, 13	ʊ	put	28
b	bad	8, 14	ɜ:	bird	29
t	tea	9, 17	ɑ:	car	29
d	did	9, 17	eɪ	page	30
k	cat	10	ɪə	near	31
g	get	10	eə	there	31
l	leg	11, 12	aɪ	five	32
r	ring	11, 12	ɔɪ	boy	32
j	yes	5	aʊ	now	32
w	wet	14			
m	me	15			
ŋ	thing	15			
n	no	12, 15			
h	hand	7			

Language chart

This chart shows which *units*, and which *tasks* within units, are useful for speakers of particular languages. The word 'all' under a unit heading shows that all the tasks in that unit are useful; numbers under a unit heading refer to the tasks which are relevant.

e.g. $\begin{smallmatrix} 1 & 3 \\ 4 & 5 \end{smallmatrix}$ means that tasks 1, 3, 4, and 5 are useful.

Language \ Unit	1 /ɪ/e/	2 /s/ʃ/	3 /ʃ/tʃ/	4 /tʃ/dʒ/ /ʒ/	5 /j/dʒ/	6 /s/z/	7 /h/	8 /p/b/	9 /t/d/	10 /k/g/	11 /l/r/
French	all		all	1 2 3 5			all				
Spanish	all	all	all	1 3 4 5	all	all					
Italian	all			4 5		all	all				
Portuguese		all		1 2 3 5	all	all					
German	all			1 3 4 5	all	3		all	all	all	
Dutch	all	all	all	all	all			all	all	all	
Scandinavian languages		all	all	all	all	all		all	all	all	
Greek	all	all	all	all	all						
Japanese	all	all		4 5		3		all	all	all	all
Chinese (Cantonese)	all		all	all	all	all		all	all	all	all
Arabic	all			1 3 4 5	all				all		
Farsi	all										
Slavonic languages	all					3		all	all	all	
N. Indian languages		all		4 5							
Tamil	all	all	all	all	all	all	all	all	all	all	

Language \ Unit	12 /l/n/ /r/	13 /v/f/ /p/	14 /b/v/ /w/	15 /n/ŋ/ /m/	16 /θ/s/ /ð/z/	17 /θ/t/ /ð/d/	18 /θ/f/ /ð/v/	19 Clusters 1	20 Clusters 2	21 Linking	22 /ə/
French				1 5 6 7	all	1 2 3 5	all				all
Spanish			1 3 5	all	1 4 5	1 3 4 5	4 5	2 4	all		all
Italian				1 5 6 7	all	all	all		all		all
Portuguese			1 3 5	1 5 6 7	all	all	all	2 4	all		2 3
German		1–4 6	1 3 4 5		all	all	all			all	2 3
Dutch		1–4 6	1 3 4 5		all	all	all			all	2 3
Scandinavian languages			1 3 4 5		all	all	all			all	2 3
Greek			1 3 4 5	1 5 6 7				4	all		all
Japanese	1 2 4 5 6		1 2 3 5					all	all		all
Chinese (Cantonese)	all		all		all	all	all	all	all		all
Arabic		all		1 5 6 7	all	all	all	all	all	all	all
Farsi			1 3 4 5	1 5 6 7	all	all	all	all	all	all	all
Slavonic languages		1–4	4 5	1 5 6 7	all	all	all		all		all
N. Indian languages		all	1 3 4 5	1 5 6 7	all	all	all	all	all		all
Tamil		1 3–6	all	1 5 6 7	all	all	all	all	all	all	all

Unit / Language	23 /iː/ɪ/	24 /æ/e/	25 /ʌ/æ/	26 /ɒ/ɔː/	27 /əʊ/ɔː/	28 /uː/ʊ/	29 /ɜː/ɑː/	30 /eɪ/e/	31 /eə/ɪə/	32 /aɪ/ɔɪ/ /aʊ/
French	all	all	all		all	all	1 2 4	1 3		
Spanish	all	all	all	all	all	all	all			
Italian	all	all	all		all	all	1 2 4			
Portuguese	all	all	all	all	all	all	1 2 4			
German		all	all							
Dutch		all	all							
Scandinavian languages			all							
Greek	all	all	all	all	all	all	1 2 4			
Japanese	all	all	all		all	all	all			
Chinese (Cantonese)	all			all	all	all	all	all		
Arabic	all	all	all	all	all	all	1 2 4			
Farsi	all	all	all	all		all	all			
Slavonic languages	all	all	all	all	all	all	1 2 4			
N. Indian languages		all	all	all		all	all	all		
Tamil		all	all	all	all	all	all	all		

Intonation list

For each intonation pattern practised in the book, there is a brief explanation, and a list of the *units* and *tasks* in the book in which it is to be found.

Stress on important words

Stressed words convey most of the information. Stressed syllables occur at regular intervals, with unstressed syllables fitting in between. Stress and intonation are closely linked.

    Unit 7 /h/ Task 3.4 page 45
    Unit 9 /t, d/ Task 3 page 50

Fall on complete, definite statement

The most common intonation pattern in English. It occurs in context throughout, and is focussed upon in the following units:

    Unit 8 /p, b/ Task 2.2 page 47
    Unit 27 /əʊ, ɔː/ Task 2.2 page 104

Wh-questions

The voice often falls in questions beginning with 'When, Where, Why, What,' etc.

    Unit 7 /h/ Tasks 2 and 3.3 pages 43 and 44
    Unit 10 /k, g/ Task 3 page 53 (mixed with Yes/No questions)
    Unit 14 /b, v, w/ Task 4 page 65
    Unit 25 /ʌ, æ/ Task 2 page 97
    Unit 29 /ɜː, ɑː/ Task 2 pages 109 and 110
    Unit 31 /eə, ɪə/ Task 4 page 117

Yes/No questions

The voice usually rises in questions to which the answer is 'Yes' or 'No'.

    Unit 6 /s, z/ Task 4 page 42
    Unit 10 /k, g/ Task 3 page 53 (mixed with Wh-questions)
    Unit 12 /l, n, r/ Task 6b page 60

Alternative questions

e.g. Does John come from Leeds or Manchester?

The speaker mentions two possible answers. The voice rises on the first alternative, and falls on the second. The two possible answers may be single words, as above, or longer phrases:

e.g. Are you going to buy a new radio or repair the old one?

    Unit 5 /j, dʒ/ Task 4.2 page 39
    Unit 9 /t, d/ Task 4.1 page 51
    Unit 18 /θ, f, ð, v/ Task 2 page 76
    Unit 30 /eɪ, e/ Task 2.2 page 114

Question tags – falling

e.g. It's a nice day, isn't it?

The speaker is certain of what he/she says. He/She expects the other person to agree with him/her. The voice falls on the question tag.

Question tags – rising

e.g. It's Tuesday today, isn't it?

The speaker is not certain. He/She is asking for confirmation. The voice rises on the question tag.

Echo questions

The speaker repeats something said by another person:

1 while he/she thinks what to reply

e.g. A: Have we got any postcards?

B: Postcards? Yes, They are in the drawer with the envelopes.

2 to query what the other person said, ask for further explanation

e.g. A: Every cook should have a computer.

B: A computer?

A: Yes, to keep a record of menus and recipes.

3 because he/she did not hear or understand or believe what was said

e.g. A: The new manager is coming tomorrow. His name is Sprot.

B: What's his name?

Correcting

1 The voice falls on the correct word, to emphasise it.

    e.g. A: Her birthday is on the tenth of December.

        B: No, it's on the fifth of December.

    Unit 5 /j, dʒ/ Task 2.2 page 38
    Unit 15 /n, ŋ, m/ Task 4 page 68
    Unit 16 /θ, s, ð, z/ Task 3 page 71
    Unit 20 Consonant clusters 2 Task 6 page 84
    Unit 23 /iː, ɪ/ Task 3.2 page 93

2 The voice falls and rises on the incorrect information, then falls on the correct information, to emphasise it.

    e.g. Her birthday isn't the tenth of December. It's the fifth.

    Unit 30 /eɪ, e/ Task 2.1 page 113

Listing

The voice rises on each item of the list, until the final one, where it falls.

e.g. She bought some potatoes, some peas, and some peaches.

    Unit 2 /s, ʃ/ Task 3c page 30
    Unit 25 /ʌ, æ/ Task 4.2 page 99
    Unit 26 /ɒ, ɔː/ Task 2b page 101

Polite rise

Because a rise sounds less definite than a fall, it can be used to sound polite, especially when beginning a conversation. It is common when answering the phone.

e.g. 'Cavendish Manufacturing Company.'

    Unit 3 /ʃ, tʃ/ Task 4.2 page 33
    Unit 20 Consonant clusters 2 Task 3 page 83
    Unit 24 /æ, e/ Task 2 page 94

Yes/No short answers

e.g. Yes, it was.

The voice often falls on 'Yes', which could be a complete answer, and also on 'it was', which is also a complete, definite statement. The speaker often goes on to give a more detailed answer, also with a fall.

    Unit 6 /s, z/ Task 4.2 page 42
    Unit 12 /l, n, r/ Task 6b page 60
    Unit 24 /æ, e/ Task 3.2 page 95

Rise in subordinate clause or non-final phrase, fall in main clause

e.g. Before I read this book, I thought stress was an executive disease.

One day, our teacher asked us to write a story.

Unit 13 /v, f, p/ Task 5.2 page 63
Unit 17 /θ, t, ð, d/ Task 4 page 74

Statement implying 'but .....'

The voice falls and rises. The fall marks the important information; the rise implies that though the speaker may have made a positive statement, he/she is going to qualify it. He/She may actually *say* 'but .....' or may simply imply it.

e.g. A: Did you have a good holiday?

B: The weather was very good. (but everything else was awful).

Unit 18 /θ, f, ð, v/ Task 4 page 78

Introductory unit
/ɪ/ if   /e/ egg

T A S K 1   Distinguish between /ɪ/ and /e/

1.1   **Listen, and practise the difference.**

pig	peg	miss	mess
hid	head	pit	pet
fill	fell	lift	left
middle	medal	sit	set
chick	cheque	lid	lead

1.2   **Listen to the words on the cassette. Write the words you hear.**

1.3   **Listen to the sentences on the cassette. For each one, write the word you hear.**

1 I'm waiting for the bill/bell.
2 Whose pin/pen is that?
3 He had tin/ten boxes.
4 She gave me a chick/cheque.
5 The lid/lead has been stolen.
6 The hidden will/well was discovered.

T A S K 2   Say /ɪ/

2a   **Listen, and practise.**

This week's interview – Tim Fitzwilliam

Our visitor this evening is the film director, Tim Fitzwilliam, this year's winner of the 'Silver Wings' film prize. His prize-winning film, *Dinner at the Ritz*, is set in India. Tim lived in India till he was sixteen, and still visits India frequently. The fifth son of an Irish father and an Indian mother, he is an Irish citizen, but lives in England.

S P E L L I N G

/ɪ/ if

Common:
i (*'short i'*):
   if, film, his
e *in verb endings
   and plurals:*
   started, dances

Less common:
e decide, English,
   women

Exceptions:
o women
u busy
a village

/e/ egg

Common:
e (*'short e'*):
   egg, editor
   bet, went

Less common:
ea dead, breath

Exceptions:
ie friend
a any, ate,
   says, said
u bury
ei leisure

COMMENTARY

TASK 1

1.1 Listen to the pairs of words in 1.1 as often as you need to. If you cannot hear the difference, listen again, another day. Concentrate hard, and listen again and again, until you begin to hear the difference. When you can *hear* the sound contrast clearly, practise *saying* the words.

1.2 On the cassette, you hear one word from the pairs of words in 1.1. You have to identify which word it is. The correct words are given in the Key. If you cannot do 1.2, at first, leave it until you have had further listening practice.

If you want further practice in identifying sounds, you may want to use Task 1.2 more than once. If you just play it several times, you begin to remember which word comes next, without recognising the sound. To avoid this, wind the tape on a little way, and play a word or sentence at random. Wind back or forward to pick out words in a different order. You might play, d) a) f) h) b) e) g). You can still use the key to check the word on the tape.

1.3 Here, you have to identify a word in the context of a sentence. Afterwards you can practise saying the pairs of sentences, e.g.

I'm waiting for the bill.
I'm waiting for the bell.

Occasionally, there may be a word you do not know. For pronunciation practice, it doesn't matter if you don't know the word; of course you can look it up afterwards to find out its meaning.

TASK 2

2a This text has lots of words with the /ɪ/ sound. Listen to the text first. You can do this with the book open or closed, as you wish. You will find it helpful sometimes to listen and underline words containing the sound you are practising. Another approach which you could use sometimes is to *read* the text silently, and underline all the words with /ɪ/. Then listen to it, and notice these words especially.

When you have listened to the text, practise saying it yourself. You can listen and repeat, phrase by phrase. Then practise it until it is as good as you can make it. If you can, record it, and listen carefully to yourself.

2b Listen to these sentences with rising question tags. The speaker isn't sure. He's asking the other person to confirm.

Tim Fitzwilliam isn't En**g**lish, **is** he?

He **won** the Silver **Wings fi**lm prize, **di**dn't he?

Now ask and answer these questions.

He isn't a film actor, is he?
He came to England when he was sixteen, didn't he?
His film is called *Dinner at the Ritz*, isn't it?
The film isn't set in England, is it?
Fitzwilliam isn't an English name, is it?
He isn't a British citizen, is he?

T A S K 3   Say /e/

Personality Test.
How often do you do the things in the chart below –
1 every time?   2 often?   3 sometimes?   4 not very often?
5 never?
Fill in the chart for yourself, then ask three other people.

	You			
memory remember your friends' birthdays remember the endings of books you have read remember what you ate for breakfast yesterday				
stress sleep well get depressed in wet weather				
family write letters to your relatives telephone them lend money to members of your family				

Now tell the rest of the class what you found.

e.g. Giovanni has a very good memory. He remembers his friends' birthdays every time. Yuko can't remember the endings of books she has read, but she can remember what she had for breakfast yesterday, because she has a boiled egg every day!

COMMENTARY

2b This is an exercise in intonation – the 'tune' of the voice. The arrows show where the voice falls and rises. In this case, the voice rises on the question tag. Listen carefully, and try to produce exactly the same intonation. Stressed syllables are shown in **bold** type. Try to make them sound stronger and louder than the syllables around them.

Practise the questions in the book, with good intonation, and strong stressed syllables. You might find it helpful to mark the stressed syllables, and to draw arrows to remind you where the voice falls and rises. Answer the questions, using information from the text. If you are working on your own, you can answer your own questions.

If you look under *Question tags – rising* in the Intonation list on page 19, you can find more exercises with this sort of question.

TASK 3

This task practises the sound /e/. If you wish, you can underline the words with /e/ before you start.

This is an example of an exercise which tells you to ask other people questions. Students working in a class can do that. If you are by yourself, you can't ask other people. But don't worry. The exercise is still useful for you. Ask yourself the questions, and answer them. Then practise saying something about yourself.

e.g. I think I've got quite a good memory – except that I can never remember telephone numbers. My stress level isn't very high; I sleep well, and don't get depressed. I very seldom write letters, because I see several of my relatives every day. I wouldn't mind lending money, but I haven't got any money to lend.

Similarly, if there is an exercise with a topic for discussion, you can say what you think.

As you see, in many exercises you don't just repeat what you have heard. You may have to answer questions, or make your own conversation, or express your own ideas. So you have to think what to say – but still make the sounds correctly! It may be helpful to record yourself, and listen to the sounds you made. Then say it again, and try to make it even better.

T A S K 4   Say /ɪ/ and /e/

4.1 **Listen, and say these phrases.**

English weather	red scissors
thrilling tennis	healthy living
guilty men	expensive gifts
silly questions	excellent singing

4.2a Listen, and practise this conversation.

A: Where were you on Wednesday? I telephoned, but you weren't in.
B: I went to Wimbledon, to watch the tennis competition.
A: Did you enjoy yourself?
B: Yes, I did. The weather wasn't very good, but the tennis was thrilling.

4.2b Make similar conversations, using the points below.

**

swimming
to the cinema
to an English lesson
to buy a leather coat

made me feel healthy.
the best film I've ever seen.
terrible!
too heavy, and very expensive.

4.2c Listen to the questions, and notice the intonation. Then ask and answer the questions.

1 **Where** did B go? **When** did she go there?

2 Did B enjoy herself?

  Did A go to Wimbledon as well?

3 Did A write to B or telephone her?

  What do they play at Wimbledon – tennis or football?

4.2d A told a friend about his conversation with B. He got some of the information wrong. Listen, and repeat what he said. Then say each thing correctly.

B went to Wimbledon on Tuesday.
Wimbledon is a football competition.
B had a terrible day.
The weather was excellent.

F U R T H E R   P R A C T I C E

/ɪ/ Unit 23:3,4 page 92–93   /e/ Unit 24:3,4 page 95–96; Unit 30:3 page 114

COMMENTARY

TASK 4

This task brings together the two sounds which have been practised separately in Tasks 2 and 3.

4.1 Some units contain a short task like this. These phrases are useful if you find it difficult to say the two sounds close together. If you want more practice, you can make up your own phrases.

4.2a Listen and practise, following the advice for Task 2.

The short conversation in 4.2a is followed up by three exercises. These show you three important types of exercise which are often used in other units. Where one exercise is based on a previous one, it has the same number. So 4.2b, 4.2c and 4.2d are all based on 4.2a.

4.2b Making similar conversations.

The symbol ** means that one side of the conversation is recorded on the cassette: you can say the other side of the conversation, using the points given in the book. You can rewind and play it several times, to make several different conversations.

In other cases, you can say both sides of the conversation yourself. You may find it helpful to underline the part of the conversation which will change each time.

4.2c Asking and answering questions.

If the exercise is marked **, the questions are on tape, for you to answer. Otherwise, you should ask *and* answer the questions. Exercises usually concentrate on one form of question, and show the intonation required. In the Intonation list on page 18, there are brief explanations and examples of the question forms practised.

4.2d Correcting wrong information.

This gives you more practice in saying the sounds. Intonation is important here; the voice falls to emphasise the correct information.

(B went to Wimbledon on Tuesday.) **B** went to **Wim**bledon on W**e**dnesday.

(Wimbledon is a football competition.) **Wim**bledon is a t**e**nnis competition.

FURTHER PRACTICE

For further practice of e.g. /ɪ/, look at Unit 23 Tasks 3 and 4 on pages 92 and 93.

/s/ so   /ʃ/ shop

T A S K 1   Distinguish between /s/ and /ʃ/

1.1   **Listen, and practise the difference.**

see	she	sock	shock
sell	shell	saw	shore
said	shed	sew	show
save	shave	Sue	shoe
mess	mesh	sort	short
Paris	parish	puss	push
ass	ash	rust	rushed
fist	fished	crust	crushed

1.2   **Listen to the words on the cassette. Write the words you hear.**

1.3   **Listen to the sentences on the cassette. For each one, write the word you hear.**

1 She's always giving me socks/shocks.
2 The sack/shack is full of rubbish.
3 That seat/sheet is dirty.
4 They're sifting/shifting the flour.
5 We took a sip/ship.
6 Could you sign/shine this please?

T A S K 2   Say /s/

2.1   **Listen, and read out these extracts from a magazine.**

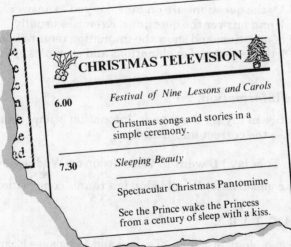

CHRISTMAS TELEVISION

6.00   *Festival of Nine Lessons and Carols*

Christmas songs and stories in a simple ceremony.

7.30   *Sleeping Beauty*

Spectacular Christmas Pantomime

See the Prince wake the Princess from a century of sleep with a kiss.

S P E L L I N G

/s/ so

ALL **s** *at the beginning of words:* see, side

ALL **ss** cross, fussy *(Exceptions:* scissors, po**ss**ess)

ALL **s** + *consonant:* stay, last

MOST **ce** centre
      ci science
      cy cycle, juicy

SOME **s** *in the middle of words:* basic, mason

SOME **se** *at the end of words:* mouse, cease

SOME **s** *at the end of words:* bus, gas

ALL *plural and 3rd person singular* **s** *after voiceless sound:* cats, writes

/ʃ/ shop

See page 31.

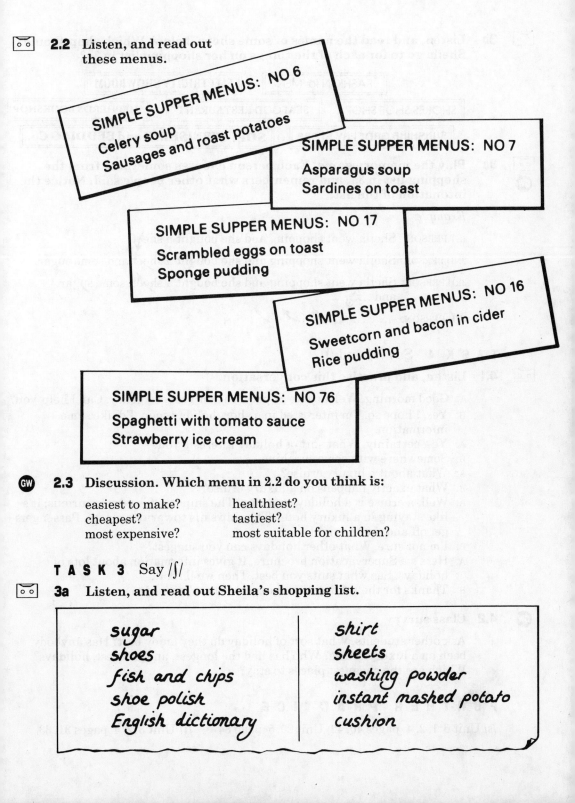

2.2 Listen, and read out these menus.

> **SIMPLE SUPPER MENUS: NO 6**
> Celery soup
> Sausages and roast potatoes

> **SIMPLE SUPPER MENUS: NO 7**
> Asparagus soup
> Sardines on toast

> **SIMPLE SUPPER MENUS: NO 17**
> Scrambled eggs on toast
> Sponge pudding

> **SIMPLE SUPPER MENUS: NO 16**
> Sweetcorn and bacon in cider
> Rice pudding

> **SIMPLE SUPPER MENUS: NO 76**
> Spaghetti with tomato sauce
> Strawberry ice cream

2.3 Discussion. Which menu in 2.2 do you think is:

easiest to make?   healthiest?
cheapest?   tastiest?
most expensive?   most suitable for children?

T A S K 3 Say /ʃ/

3a Listen, and read out Sheila's shopping list.

> sugar
> shoes
> fish and chips
> shoe polish
> English dictionary
>
> shirt
> sheets
> washing powder
> instant mashed potato
> cushion

3b Listen, and read the names of some shops, below. Which shop should Sheila go to for each of the things on her shopping list in 3a?

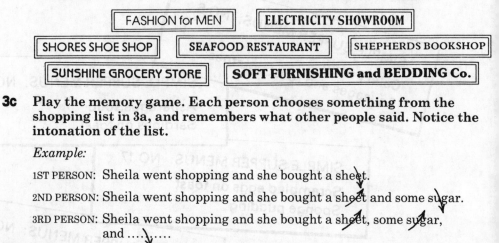

| FASHION for MEN | | ELECTRICITY SHOWROOM |

SHORES SHOE SHOP   SEAFOOD RESTAURANT   SHEPHERDS BOOKSHOP

SUNSHINE GROCERY STORE   SOFT FURNISHING and BEDDING Co.

3c Play the memory game. Each person chooses something from the shopping list in 3a, and remembers what other people said. Notice the intonation of the list.

Example:

1ST PERSON: Sheila went shopping and she bought a sheet.

2ND PERSON: Sheila went shopping and she bought a sheet and some sugar.

3RD PERSON: Sheila went shopping and she bought a sheet, some sugar, and ....

4TH PERSON: ....

TASK 4 Say /s/ and /ʃ/

4.1 Listen, and practise this conversation.

A: Good morning. Welcome to Supervacation Travel Agency. Can I help you?
B: Yes, I hope so. I'm interested in a short holiday soon. I'd like some information.
A: Yes, certainly. What sort of holiday interests you?
B: Somewhere with some sunshine.
A: What about a luxury cruise?
B: What exactly happens on a luxury cruise?
A: Well, a cruise is a holiday on a ship. The ship itself is very luxurious; it's like staying in a luxury hotel. The ship sails to various places. Passengers get off and see the sights.
B: I'm not sure. What other holidays can you suggest?
A: Here's a Supervacation brochure. It gives information about lots of holidays. See what suits you best. Then we'll fix it.
B: Thanks for the information. I expect I'll see you soon.

4.2 Class survey

Ask other students. What sort of holiday do they enjoy best? Has anybody been on a luxury cruise? Who has had the longest, and shortest, holidays? Which are the cheapest places to stay?

FURTHER PRACTICE

/s/ Unit 6:1, 2, 4 pages 40, 42; Unit 20:5 page 84   /ʃ/ Unit 3:2, 4 pages 31, 33

TASK 1   Distinguish between /ʃ/ and /tʃ/

1.1   Listen, and practise the difference.

ship	chip	washing	watching
sherry	cherry	cash	catch
shoes	choose	mash	match
sheep	cheap	wish	which, witch
share	chair	crush	crutch
shops	chops	dishes	ditches

1.2   Listen to the words on the cassette.
Write the words you hear.

1.3   Listen to the sentences on the cassette.
For each one, write the word you hear.

1 Small shops/chops are often expensive.
2 The dishes/ditches need cleaning.
3 I couldn't mash/match these things up.
4 She enjoys washing/watching the children.

TASK 2   Say /ʃ/

Below are some extracts from advertisements. With a partner work out which pieces go together. (Then you can listen to the cassette to check.)

Improve your education

with Bishops special shoe polish

Feel fresh after your shave –

Advertise in *Musicians' Weekly*

Make your shoes shine

the freshest fish in town

Are you a musician with ambition?

with the *Shorter English Dictionary* – new edition

It's new!   It's smashing!

use FRESH aftershave lotion

Straight from the ship to the shop –

CRASH – the new instant mashed potato

T A S K 3 Say /tʃ/

3.1 Listen, and say these phrases, with /tʃ/ after /t/. Link the words together, to help you say /tʃ/ correctly.

It's quite cheap   Don't cheat

a white chair   a great chance

a hot cheese sandwich   a fat child

3.2 Listen, and say these phrases. Be careful to say /tʃ/. (It may help to think of a small 't' before the 'ch'.)

It's very cheap.   You cheat!
a grey chair   no chance
a cheese sandwich   a pretty child

3.3a Listen, and practise the conversation.

A: Which flat shall we choose?
B: Well, the one in Churchill Square had a lovely kitchen. But the one in Church Street was cheaper.
A: Yes, Church Street was much cheaper. Never mind the kitchen. Let's choose the cheap one!

3.3b Make similar conversations using the notes below.

HOTELS – in South Beach Road – near the beach
         next to the church – cheap

EMPLOYERS – Mr Chandos – charming
          – Mr Champion – rich

PRESENT FOR A CHILD – watch – teach him to tell the time
                    – chess set – enjoyable

FLIGHTS – Channel Airways – more choice
        – charter company – cheap

TASK 4   Say /ʃ/ and /tʃ/

4.1   **How much do you enjoy the things in the chart below –**
1 very much?   2 not much?   3 not at all?
Fill in the chart for yourself, then ask three other people.

	You			
playing chess watching TV washing up going to a football match cooking chips eating chips lying in the sunshine shopping				

Now tell the rest of the class what you found.

e.g. Maria doesn't like watching TV much. Jean and David like watching
TV, but they don't like washing up.

4.2a   **Listen, and practise this conversation in a shop. Notice the shop**
assistant's polite, rising intonation.

A: Can I help you?

B: Yes, I'm looking for some cheap shoes.

A: The ones on that shelf are quite cheap.

B: No thank you. They're too shiny.

A: Would you like to choose some from this shelf, then?

B: Right ..... I've chosen these.

A: Would you like to pay cash or by cheque?

B: Cash, please.

4.2b   **Make similar conversations. B can choose things from below.**
**

some cheap shirts
some cheap sheets
some cheap shorts

They're too short.
I don't like the shade.
I don't like the shape.

cash
cheque

FURTHER PRACTICE

/ʃ/ Unit 2:3, 4 pages 29–30
/tʃ/ Unit 4:2, 4, 5 pages 34–36

/tʃ/ chin   /dʒ/ judge
/ʒ/ pleasure

T A S K 1   Distinguish between /tʃ/ and /dʒ/

1.1   **Listen, and practise the difference.**

chin	gin	rich	ridge
cheer	jeer	search	surge
choke	joke	H	age
chain	Jane	larch	large

1.2   **Listen to the words on the cassette.**
Write the words you hear.

1.3   **Listen to the sentences on the cassette.**
For each one, write the word you hear.

1 Look out. He's choking/joking.
2 The audience cheered/jeered at her speech.
3 It's not a little fir tree, it's a larch/large tree.
4 What happened to your chin/gin?

T A S K 2   Say /tʃ/

2a   **Listen, and practise this conversation.**

A: Can you play chess?
B: Yes, I enjoy chess very much. I was a chess
    champion when I was a child.
A: And are you still a champion chess player?
B: No, things have changed. In my last match I was
    beaten by a seven-year-old child. I think she's a
    future champion!

2b   **Listen to these sentences with question tags.**
The speaker isn't sure. She's asking the other
person to confirm.

You can **play chess**, can't you?

You were a **chess champion**, weren't you?

Now say these sentences, adding question tags.

You're still a champion chess player,
You were beaten by a seven-year-old child,
You think she's a future champion,

T A S K 3   Say /dʒ/

3a   **Listen, and practise this conversation.**

A: Hello, Janice Jones speaking.
B: Hello, Janice. This is John Johnson. Is Jenny in?
A: No, she's not. Can I take a message?
B: Yes, please. Tell her that I've got her luggage. Could she collect it?

3b   Read the message below, which Janice wrote.

> *Jenny*
> *John rang. Please collect your luggage.*
>   *Janice*

(PW) **3c**   Below are two more notes. With a partner, make up a conversation
which took place before each note was written.

> *Jane*
>
> *Your mother left a message. Please
> buy a large cabbage and some
> orange juice.*
>   *Jack*

> *Jennifer*
>
> *I've just heard from Josephine. She can't
> meet you tonight, as arranged. She's had
> a car accident. She's not injured, but
> the car engine is damaged.*
>   *Gerald*

T A S K   4 Say /ʒ/

4a   Listen, and practise this conversation.

A: Did you watch *Treasure Island* on television yesterday?
B: No, I watched a programme called *Leisure Time*.

(PW) **4b**   Make similar conversations about these television programmes.

**
Measure for Measure   *Reading for Pleasure*   *Casualty*
The Color Purple and the Colour Beige   *Vision of the Future*

T A S K 5   Say /tʃ/ and /dʒ/ and /ʒ/

5a   **Listen, and practise this telephone conversation.**

A: Leisure and Pleasure General Stores. Can I help you?

B: Good morning. There's something wrong with my television. Could you arrange to repair it?

A: How long have you had the television?

B: I bought it in January.

A: What's the problem?

B: The picture keeps jumping.

A: Just a moment. Our engineer is free on Tuesday, after lunch.

B: Could you manage something sooner? I want to watch television before Tuesday.

A: I'll put it down as an urgent repair. The engineer usually calls in at lunchtime. I'll try and catch him then.

5b   **Make similar conversations, using the information from the report sheet below.**

**

Leisure and Pleasure General Stores
REPORT SHEET ON REPAIRS REQUESTED

Item	Problem	Month of purchase	Urgent
TV	Picture keeps jumping	January	Yes – owner wants to watch it!
car	engine makes an unusual noise	July	Yes – owner is making a long journey next week
watch	got damaged – dropped on kitchen floor	June	Yes – owner is a teacher; needs a watch
fridge	it flashes when touched	July	Yes – switched off now; fridge is full of food
washing machine	nothing happens when switched on	January	Yes – owner has 5 children!

F U R T H E R   P R A C T I C E

/tʃ/ Unit 3:3, 4 pages 32–33   /dʒ/ Unit 5:3, 4 pages 38–39

/j/ yes /dʒ/ judge

TASK 1 Distinguish between /j/ and /dʒ/

1.1 Listen, and practise the difference.

yet	jet	yam	jam
use (*n*)	juice	yolk, yoke	joke
yak	Jack	year	jeer
yeti	jetty	yes	Jess

1.2 Listen to the words on the cassette. Write the words you hear.

1.3 Listen to the sentences on the cassette. For each one, write the word you hear.

1 He's cooking something odd, with yam/jam in it.
2 All the yolks/jokes were bad.
3 The years/jeers have gone by.
4 She says she saw a yeti/jetty when she was on holiday.

TASK 2 Say /j/

2.1 Listen, and read out the titles of these television programmes.

EUROVISION SONG CONTEST

[illegible]

THE YOUNG ONES

[illegible]

NEW YORK, NEW YORK

[illegible]

YELLOW SUBMARINE

[illegible]

A YORKSHIRE VET

[illegible]

NEW YEAR CELEBRATIONS

[illegible]

A DOCUMENTARY

a documentary about trade unions

ABOUT COMPUTERS

a documentary about computers for young people

EUROPEAN YOUTH

European Youth Orchestra

UNIVERSITY CHALLENGE

(a quiz programme for students)

SPELLING

/j/ yes

ALL **y** *at the beginning of words:* yellow, you

Before SOME **u** *at the beginning of words:* university, use

Before SOME /uː/ *after some consonants:* beautiful, *due, few, argue, Kew, queue, music, *new, pure, *tune

*In words marked *, /j/ is omitted by American speakers.*

Exception: Europe

/dʒ/ judge

ALL **j** jam, job

ALL **g** *before* **e**: general, manage

ALL **dge** judge

SOME **g** *before* **i** ginger, imagine

2.2a **Listen, and practise this conversation.**

> A: How do English universities choose students?
> B: You usually apply to four universities. The universities may interview you. They usually refuse to take students who fail their end-of-year exams.
> A: Have you applied for university yet?
> B: Yes, and I heard from York University yesterday. I've got an interview next week.

2.2b **Listen, and practise correcting incorrect statements. Notice how the voice falls to emphasise the correct information.**

You **u**sually ap**ply** to **three** uni**ver**sities.

No, you **u**sually ap**ply** to **fo**ur uni**ver**sities.

The uni**ver**sities **must in**terview you.

No, the universities **may in**terview you.

** **Now correct these statements.**

> B   has not applied for university.
> B   has heard from Sussex University.
> B   heard from the university today.
> B   has got an interview tomorrow.

TASK 3   Say /dʒ/

3.1a **Listen, and say these jobs.**

> judge   jockey   general   baggage-handler
> carriage-cleaner   messenger

3.1b **Look at the list of workplaces below. Match each job with a workplace.**

e.g. A judge might work in a courtroom.

> airport   racecourse   Army headquarters   courtroom
> office   railway station

3.2a **These dates are days of celebration in some countries. Can you say what and where?**

> 6 January   4 July   14 July   1 January   21 June
> (answers on page 121)

3.2b **What do you think of when you think of these days and months?**

e.g. 'When I think of July 4th, I think of fireworks.'
     'When I think of June, I think of weddings.'

3.3   Food and drink puzzle: all the answers contain the sound /dʒ/.

1 Fruit boiled with sugar
   until it is thick.
2 The liquid part of fruit
3 An alcoholic drink
4 A green vegetable
5 A hot-tasting root used
   in cooking
6 A juicy fruit

(solution on page 121)

T A S K 4   Say /j/ and /dʒ/

4.1   Listen, and say these phrases.

a yellow jumper	a bridge in Yorkshire
a European judge	a large university
a young journalist	a damaged yacht
a useful journey	a strange youth

4.2a Listen, and practise this conversation.

A: Can I help you?
B: Yes, I'm looking for John Yardley.
A: John Yardley? Sorry, I don't know anyone here called John Yardley.
B: That's strange. He's the computer manager. I've arranged an
   appointment.
A: I think you've made a mistake. The computer manager is Jennifer Young.
B: Oh! This is the office of Youth and Computers, isn't it?
A: No. This is the General Workers Union ..... Youth and Computers is
   next door.

4.2b Listen to these alternative questions. Notice the intonation.
Then ask and answer the questions.

Is B looking for **John Yardley** or **Jennifer Young**?

B mentions a **job**. Is it **sales** director or computer **manager**?

Does B **want Youth** and Computers or the **General Workers Union**?

Are they in the **office** of **Youth** and Computers or the **General Workers**
Union?

Is the **office** of **Youth** and Computers **opposite** or **next door**?

F U R T H E R P R A C T I C E

/dʒ/ Unit 4:3, 4, 5 pages 34–36

UNIT 6 /s/ so /z/ zoo

TASK 1 Distinguish between /s/ and /z/

1.1 Listen, and practise the difference.

Sue	zoo	rice	rise
said	Zed	loose	lose
seal	zeal	race	raise
lacy	lazy	advice	advise
fussy	fuzzy	once	ones
sip	zip	lice	lies

1.2 Listen to the words on the cassette. Write the words you hear.

1.3 Listen to the sentences on the cassette. For each one, write the word you hear.

1 We're hoping for peace/peas.
2 The price/prize was wonderful.
3 It was full of lice/lies.
4 Be careful, don't sip/zip it too fast.
5 She heard a bus/buzz.
6 He only has a few pence/pens left.

TASK 2 Say /s/

2a Listen, and practise this weather forecast.

Temperatures are expected to fall to minus six degrees in the south. Northern areas will have severe frost, with snow on the hills. It may also snow near the south coast. Roads will be icy – drive slowly, and don't get too close to other cars. Watch out for patches of freezing fog. Don't drive too fast – it's dangerous in these conditions.

* Frost

* Freezing fog

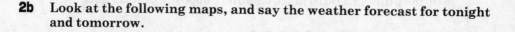

Sun

Snow

Ice or Icy roads

2b Look at the following maps, and say the weather forecast for tonight and tomorrow.

SPELLING

/s/ so
See page 28.

/z/ zoo

ALL **z** zoo, freeze
SOME **s** *in the middle of words:* music, pleasant
SOME **se** *at the end of words:* choose, ease
SOME **s** *at the end of words:* was, has
ALL *plural and 3rd person singular* **s** *after voiced sound:* dogs, adds

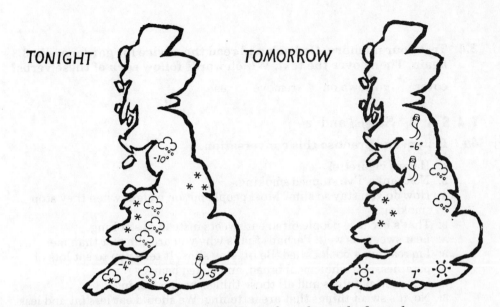

TONIGHT   TOMORROW

T A S K 3   Say /z/ in the middle and at the end of words

3.1   **Listen, and say these pairs of words with /z/.**

easy	Isaac	rising	Caesar	razor
ease	eyes	rise	seize	raise

fuzzy	fizzy	freezer	lazy	crazy
fuzz	fizz	freeze	laze	craze

3.2   **Listen, and say these clues. Match them with words from 3.1.**

It's used for shaving.   Turn water into ice.
The sun does this in the east.   The opposite of 'release'.
Used for seeing.   The opposite of 'sane'.
Julius was a famous one.   The opposite of 'difficult'.
Doesn't like hard work.

3.3   **Listen, and practise.**

Advice for gardeners

This season, I advise you to do two easy things:
use your eyes, and go down on your knees!

First, use your eyes: look at weather conditions.
Clear skies often bring freezing winds. Cover
your plants, or you will lose them.

Second, go down on your knees, so you can
really see your plants. See if there are signs of
disease on the leaves. If there are, remove the
diseased ones.

3.4   Test your memory. Go back and read the advice for gardeners in 3.3
again. Then cover the text. Which words follow each of these verbs?

cover   go down on   remove   use

T A S K 4   Say /s/ and /z/

4a   Listen, and practise this conversation.

A: Have a cigarette!
B: No thanks. I've stopped smoking.
A: How do you stay so slim? Most people put on weight when they stop
    smoking.
B: That's because people often eat sweets instead of smoking.
A: I eat sweets as well! Perhaps that's why you are slimmer than me.
B: I'm reading a book called 'Be fit, stay slim'. It tells you to eat lots of
    potatoes, and wholemeal bread, and baked beans.
A: I thought potatoes and all those things were fattening.
B: No, it's sweet things that are fattening. We should eat less fat and less
    sugar. The book advises eating lots of fruit.
A: That's easy in the summer. But it's not so easy in winter.
B: It's possible in winter too. You can freeze some things – frozen raspberries
    are very good. Anyway this book gives some suggested menus. Breakfast:
    cereal, two slices of toast, tea or coffee. Lunch: a cheese sandwich, and
    two small peaches.
A: It doesn't sound much. What's for supper?
B: Vegetable soup, beans on toast, and a small ice cream. I love beans on
    toast. It's so easy to make.

4b   Listen, and practise these questions and answers.

Does B **want** a cigarette? No, he **doesn't**. He's **stopped smoking**.

Has B **put on weight**? No, he **hasn't**. He's **still slim**.

Does A **eat sweets**? Yes, she **does**.

Now ask and answer these questions.

Does B like beans on toast?   Are frozen raspberries good?
Does B eat snacks?   Are potatoes fattening?
Does A eat sweets?   Should we eat more fat?

4c   Ask people about food and about smoking.

Do they like sweet things/wholemeal bread, etc.?
What sort of food do they like best?
If they smoke, have they ever tried to stop? What happened?
If they used to smoke, how did they stop?

F U R T H E R   P R A C T I C E

/s/ Unit 2:2 page 28–29   /s/z/ Unit 16:1, 3, 5 pages 70–72

/h/ hand

T A S K 1 Distinguish between /h/ and no /h/

1.1 **Listen, and practise the difference.**

hand	and	harm	arm
hall	all	hill	ill
here, hear	ear	his	is
high	I, eye	hold	old
hate	eight	hat	at
heart	art	hair	air

1.2 **Listen to the words on the cassette.**
Write the words you hear.

1.3 **Listen to the sentences on the cassette.**
For each one, write the word you hear.

1 My heart/art is the most important thing for me.
2 The hair/air is very thin.
3 It's near the hedge/edge.
4 We must heat/eat up the potatoes.

T A S K 2 Say /h/

2a **Listen, and read out this postcard.**

Dear Harriet,
I'm having a horrible
holiday here! The hotel
is huge and high up on
a hill. I hurt my heel and
had to go to hospital.
The weather's too hot,
and I'm hungry. Harry's
quite happy, however!
Next summer, I shall
stay at home. Harry
can go on holiday by
himself.
Hilary

ms Harriet Harlow
4 Hamburg House
28 Harrow Road
Harrow on the Hill
Middx
England

2b **Listen, and notice the falling intonation on these Wh-questions. Then ask and answer the questions.**

How was Hilary's holiday?

Where was the hotel?

Why did Hilary go to hospital?

What was the weather like?

How was Harry?

What will happen next summer?

TASK 3 Say /h/ in the right places

3.1 **Listen, and say these phrases.**

hurry up	at home
hold on	over here
help out	an old house
half an hour	an early holiday
heart attack	an air hostess
Holiday Inn	I can hear you

3.2a **Listen, and say these words. Notice which words have /h/ in the middle.**

anyhow   anyone   behind   beyond

3.2b **Listen to the words on the cassette. For each one, decide whether it contains /h/ in the middle.**

3.3 **Listen, and practise these conversations in a hospital emergency department. Notice the falling intonation of the doctor's Wh-questions.**

A: How can I help you?

B: I've hurt my hand.

A: How did it happen?

B: I was opening a tin. It was hard to open, and I was in a hurry. When it was half open, the tin-opener slipped. I cut my hand. There was blood everywhere. It was horrible.

———————

A: How can I help you?

B: It's my son, Anton. He's got earache. He's had it for days.

A: Let's have a look ..... Ah yes, he's got something in his ear. I'll have to get it out.

A: How can I help you?
B: I've hurt my eye.
A: How did it happen?
B: I was hammering a nail. The end of the hammer flew off, and hit me in the eye.

A: How can I help you?
B: I've hurt my ankle. I think it's broken.
A: Let's see. Does that hurt?
B: Ow! Yes, it hurts awfully.
A: How did it happen?
B: My husband left his umbrella in the hall. The handle got hooked round my ankle, and I fell over. My ankle hurt so much, I could hardly get up.
A: How did you get to the hospital? Did your husband bring you?
B: No, my husband was out. I had to have an ambulance.

A: How can I help you?
B: I've got a headache.
A: This is a hospital emergency department. A headache isn't an emergency. Go and take an aspirin.
B: But I fell off a horse. I hit my head. That's why I've got a headache. I think I ought to have an X-ray.

3.4a Look at the doctor's notes below.

Henry Amis – cut hand when opening tin
Anton Hardy – something in ear
Harriet Adler – hit in eye by hammer
Anne Herring – hurt ankle on husband's umbrella
Andrew Hall – fell off horse.

The notes contain the important information. When the doctor **says** what happened, the words containing important information are **stressed**. Other words fit in between.

3.4b Listen, and practise the example. Notice the rhythm.

Henry Amis cut his hand when he was opening a tin.

Now say what happened to each person mentioned in the doctor's notes.

UNIT 8 /p/ pen /b/ bad

T A S K 1 Distinguish between /p/ and /b/

1.1 **Listen, and practise the difference.**

pit	bit	rope	robe
pat	bat	tripe	tribe
port	bought	tap	tab
pull	bull	cup	cub
pride	bride	rip	rib

1.2 **Listen to the words on the cassette.**
Write the words you hear.

1.3 **Listen to the sentences on the cassette.**
For each one, write the word you hear.

1 Have you got a pet/bet?
2 There's a pin/bin in the corner.
3 She saw some pears/bears in the garden.
4 The peach/beach was dirty.
5 Have you seen the plays/blaze?
6 The rope/robe is too short.
7 What does 'tripe/tribe' mean?
8 The doctor looked at the rip/rib.

T A S K 2 Say /p/

2.1 **Listen, and say these questions and answers.**

How much is that pullover?
Twelve pounds seventy-five pence.

How much are those peaches?
Fifteen pence each.

How much is that map?
Ninety-five pence.

How much are those stamps?
Twenty-two pence.

Now ask and answer questions about the following things.

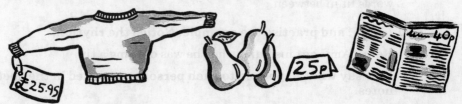

2.2a Listen and practise this conversation in a shop. Notice the intonation marked. B is making definite statements, with a fall.

A: Can I help you?

B: I hope so. I have a complaint. I bought a pullover in your shop. It was a beautiful pullover, and very expensive.

A: What happened?

B: It was a present for a friend abroad. You said you could pack it, and post it for me. I was very pleased.

A: What's the problem?

B: The parcel was damaged in the post. The paper came off. The pullover was spoilt.

A: Oh dear. I'm sorry the pullover was spoilt. But it happened in the post. So the Post Office are responsible.

B: The Post Office said that the parcel wasn't properly packed. You are responsible.

A: We are very experienced at packing parcels. Lots of people send our pullovers as presents. We wrap up hundreds of pullovers. I'm sure our parcel was properly packed.

B: I'd like to speak to the department manager, please .....

2.2b With a partner, make up B's conversation with the manager.

TASK 3 Say /b/

Listen to this quiz. Then ask a partner.

HEALTH QUIZ

a) Do you go to bed before ten?
b) Do you eat brown bread?
c) Do you put little or no butter on your bread?

d) Do you belong to a sports club?
e) Do you sleep on a hard bed?

4 or 5 YESes – Bravo!   3 YESes – Not bad, but could be better!
1 or 0 YESes – Be careful!

T A S K   4   Say /p/ and /b/

4.1   **Listen, and practise this conversation in a travel agent's.**

A: Good morning. I'd like to book a cheap spring holiday. What package holidays are available?

B: There's a splendid holiday in Paris.

A: I expect Paris is expensive!

B: There is a cheap period between November and February. You can compare our prices with other companies. Ours are cheaper.

A: But I don't want to go in February. I'd prefer April.

B: Well, April in Paris is beautiful. But it's very popular. Most package tours in April are fully booked.

A: Yes, I remember my neighbour went to Paris in April. She belongs to a travel club. It was beautiful. But the airport was very busy. What other places are available in April?

B: Here's a brochure, with all the places and prices.

A: Right, I'll probably be back tomorrow. Goodbye.

4.2a **Look at the picture. Say what you can see.**

e.g. There's some bread. There are five plates.

4.2b **Say where the things are. Use words like 'between', 'behind', 'beside', 'below', 'on top of', 'at the back'.**

e.g. There's a bottle of beer at the back.
The pans are on top of the cupboard.
The plates are below the pans.

F U R T H E R   P R A C T I C E

/p/ Unit 13:1, 5, 6 pages 61–63   /b/ Unit 14:1, 2, 5 pages 64–66

T A S K 1 Distinguish between /t/ and /d/

1.1 Listen, and practise the difference.

two	do	sight	side
ten	den	heart	hard
ton	done	plate	played
town	down	bat	bad
train	drain	set	said

1.2 Listen to the words on the cassette.
Write the words you hear.

1.3 Listen to the sentences on the cassette.
For each one, write the word you hear.

1 There was something wrong with the trains/drains.
2 She tied/dyed the scarf.
3 They saw a trunk/drunk lying on the ground.
4 He writes/rides very well.
5 This cart/card has just arrived.
6 My brother hit/hid the ball.
7 He has never made a bet/bed.

T A S K 2 Say /t/

Listen, and repeat.

Could you tell me the time, please?
It's ten to two.

Now ask and answer about these times. Remember to make the word 'to'
very weak and quick.

T A S K 3 Say /d/

3a **Read these notes, which were made during a phone call.**

> Mr Dickens phoned - Dickens Decorators Ltd.
> Goods ordered - delayed. Delivered Friday.

The notes contain the important information. When we **say** what happened, the words containing important information are stressed. Other words fit in between.

3b **Listen and practise this example. Notice the rhythm.**

'**Mr Dickens phoned** from **Dickens Decorators Limited**. The **goods** you **or**dered have been de**layed**. They will be de**livered** on **Fri**day.'

Now say in full each of the messages below.

> Diana
> David phoned -
> Shoulder bad -
> Gone to doctor.
>   Donald

> Douglas
> Duncan Dudley's deputy
> phoned. Duncan on
> holiday - Devon,
> Monday - Friday.
>   Enid

T A S K 4 Say /t/ and /d/

4.1a **Listen, and practise this conversation in a library.**

A: Good afternoon. I've just joined the library. How many books can I take out?

B: You can take two books, and keep them for ten days. After that, if you have finished them, you return them. If you haven't finished, you can renew them.

A: How do I do that? Must I visit the library?

B: No, you can telephone. Tell us the titles of the books, and the date they are due for return.

A: Splendid. Can you tell me where to find Thomas Hardy's books? I'm studying Victorian writers. I've read two of Thomas Hardy's books – *Tess of the D'Urbevilles,* and *Far from the Madding Crowd.* Today I want *A Tale of Two Cities,* or *David Copperfield.*

B: Actually *A Tale of Two Cities* and *David Copperfield* are by Charles Dickens.

4.1b Listen to these alternative questions. Notice the intonation. Then ask and answer the questions.

Can he **take** out **two books** or **ten books**?

Can he **keep** them for **two days** or **ten days**?

To re**new books, must** he **write** or **telephone**?

Is he **stud**ying Vic**tor**ian **writers** or **twenty**tieth-**century writers**?

Has he **read two books** by **Thom**as **Hardy** or **ten books**?

Is *A Tale of Two Cities* by **Thom**as **Hardy** or **Charles Dickens**?

4.2 Listen, and practise this conversation.

A: What's the matter?
B: I've hurt my toe.
A: How did it happen?
B: Somebody trod on it.
A: Put it in cold water.
 That will make it better.

Now make similar conversations about these situations.

B's problems: A's suggestions:

FURTHER PRACTICE

/t/ Unit 17:1, 2 page 73   /d/ Unit 17:1, 3, 4 pages 73–74

UNIT 10   /k/ cat   /g/ get

T A S K 1 Distinguish between /k/ and /g/

1.1 Listen, and practise the difference.

could	good		leak	league
cot	got		pick	pig
coat	goat		lock	log
cave	gave		ankle	angle
clue	glue		crow	grow

1.2 Listen to the words on the cassette.
Write the words you hear.

1.3 Listen to the sentences on the cassette.
For each one, write the word you hear.

1 One of the cards/guards is missing.
2 What a beautiful curl/girl!
3 My cold/gold has gone.
4 Sarah's class/glass is quite big.
5 There's no clue/glue.
6 I could see her back/bag in the crowded train.
7 He cut through the lock/log.

T A S K 2 Say /k/

2a Listen, and practise this conversation.

A: How many cups of tea and coffee do you drink each day?
B: I'll count them. I drink two cups of coffee at breakfast. In the morning
   break, I drink another cup of coffee. In the tea break at three o'clock, I
   have a cup of tea and a biscuit. When I get in from work, I drink a couple
   of cups of tea. And later in the evening, I drink another cup of coffee.
A: So that's four cups of coffee, and three cups of tea.
B: Yes. And if I'm working late, I have a couple of cups of coffee to keep me
   awake.

2b Say how many cups of tea and coffee you drink. Ask other people.
Tell the rest of the class.

e.g. Maria doesn't drink coffee, but she drinks a lot of tea. Sebastian drinks
one cup of tea, and about four cups of coffee.

T A S K 3 Say /g/

3a Listen, and practise this conversation.

A: I want to improve my English. Is it a good idea to go to a language school in August?
B: I went to an English summer school a year ago. It was at the Gold School of English.
A: Was it good?
B: Yes, very good. There were grammar lessons. And regular progress tests. And we also played games. That was great.
A: What sort of games?
B: Guessing games, for example. A simple game is the Bag Game. One group has a big bag, and the other group guesses what's in the bag. It's a good game at the beginning, to get to know each other.
A: Did you get to know the other students well?
B: Yes. It wasn't a big group. I've forgotten exactly how many. We got on very well together.

3b Listen to some questions about the conversation. Notice that the voice rises in the Yes/No questions, and falls in the Wh-questions.

When did B go to an **English summer school**?

What was the **school called**?

Did they **study grammar**?

What **else** did they **do**?

How do you **play** the **Bag Game**?

Did B get **on** with the **other students**?

Now ask and answer the questions.

T A S K 4 Say /k/ and /g/

4.1a Listen, and practise these sentences.

Problems	Solutions
My car's broken down.	Call an ambulance.
Cats keep coming into my garden.	Cut the grass.
My cousin has broken his leg.	Drink a cup of coffee.
I've broken a glass in the kitchen.	Call a mechanic.
There's a cow in my garden.	Look it up in the phone book.
I've been bitten by a dog.	Get a dog.
I've forgotten Carol's address.	Pick it up carefully.
I can't keep awake.	Go to the doctor.
My garden looks a mess.	Take a photograph.

4.1b Match each problem in 4.1a with a solution.

e.g. A: My car's broken down.   B: Call a mechanic.

4.2a Listen, and practise this conversation between a husband and wife.

A: I can't do all the housework and all the cooking. You've got to do more.
B: You don't do all the housework and all the cooking. I cook the breakfast.
A: And I clean the kitchen.
B: I take the dog for a walk.
A: I take the kids to school.
B: I do the gardening.
A: No you don't. I cut the grass.
B: I dig the garden.
A: Once a year, in August.
B: I make you a cup of coffee every evening.
A: I cook the supper.
B: I clean the car.
A: I pick up your things.
B: OK. Let's change over. I'll pick up my own things. And you can clean the car.
A: You can cook supper.
B: You can make the coffee.
A: You can cut the grass.
B: You can dig the garden.
A: Once a year, in August. You can take the kids to school.
B: You can take the dog for a walk.
A: You can clean the kitchen.
B: And we'll give up cooked breakfasts.

4.2b Do you do the household tasks mentioned in the conversation, or others? Which tasks do you like, or dislike? Make a list. Then tell other students. Try to find your ideal partner – someone who likes the jobs you dislike.

4.2c Discussion. Are some tasks 'women's jobs' or 'men's jobs'? Who usually does what in your country?

T A S K 1 Distinguish between /l/ and /r/

1.1 Listen, and practise the difference.

lip	rip	list	wrist
lap	rap, wrap	belly	berry
light	right	collect	correct
law	raw	alive	arrive
lead	read	long	wrong

1.2 Listen to the words on the cassette.
Write the words you hear.

1.3 Listen to the sentences on the cassette.
For each one, write the word you hear.

1 The water goes through a lead/red pipe.
2 Let go of my list/wrist.
3 She weighed the packet, and found the weight was light/right.
4 The examiner is collecting/correcting the exam papers today.
5 He dialled a long/wrong number.
6 Mr Lyon/Ryan is here.

T A S K 2 Say /l/

2.1a Listen, and say these warnings from road signs.

Turn left	Elderly people
No left turn	Height limit
Speed limit	Steep hill
No cycling	– use low gear
Low flying planes	

2.1b Match each warning with one of the pictures below.

2.2a **Listen, and practise this commentary on a guided tour.**

Ladies and gentlemen, on your left you will see Lumley Castle. This belongs to Lord and Lady Lumley, who live here with their family. All the land on the left of the road belongs to the Lumleys. They have a famous collection of wild animals, including lions, so please do not leave the coach until we are safely inside the car park. We are lucky; Lord Lumley is allowing us to leave the grounds and go inside this beautiful stately home. Most people can only look at the castle from outside. The time now is quarter to eleven. Please return to the coach by quarter past twelve. Don't be late, or we'll miss lunch.

2.2b **Listen to these echo questions. B is not sure what A said. His voice begins low, and rises.**

A: **Lumley Castle is on your left.**

B: **Where is Lumley Castle?**

A: **Lord and Lady Lumley have a collection of wild animals.**

B: **What have they got?**

(PW) **Now make echo questions about these sentences.**

✱✱

The castle belongs to Lord and Lady Lumley. (Who ..... ?)
The Lumley family live in the castle. (Where ..... ? or Who ..... ?)
We are going inside the castle. (Where ..... ?)
The time is quarter to eleven. (What ..... ?)

T A S K 3 Say /r/

3.1 **Listen, and practise this telephone conversation.**

A: Is that Richmond Travel Agency?
B: No, this is British Rail Enquiries.
A: Sorry. Wrong number.

(PW) **Now make similar conversations about these places.**

Radio Rentals	the Regency Restaurant
Robin's Record Shop	the Royal Free Hospital
Rent-A-Car	the Electricity Company
Refrigerator Retailers	the Rates Office

3.2 **Listen, and practise.**

A: Can I borrow your ruler?
B: Sorry, Ruth borrowed it yesterday, and she hasn't returned it.

(PW) **Now make similar conversations about the things and people on page 57.**

T A S K 4 Say /l/ and /r/

4.1 Listen and practise this conversation in a shop.

A: I'm looking for a raincoat, please.

B: Yes, of course. They're over here, on the left. There's been rather a rush today. Now, what about this blue one?

A: No, the blue is too bright.

B: But blue suits you.

A: Really? I think I look terrible in blue. I'd rather have a brown raincoat. There was one in the front window that was rather attractive.

B: I'm sorry, that's the only brown one left, and it's a very large size. Do you like yellow? This yellow one is the right size.

A: No, not yellow. Have you only got blue and yellow?

B: I'm afraid so. This year the fashionable colours are brown, cream, blue and yellow. The brown and cream raincoats have all been sold already, so there's only blue or yellow left.

A: Right! I think I'll try the shop across the road.

4.2a Listen, and repeat these sentences with question tags. The speaker is certain, and expects the other person to agree.

She's **look**ing for a **rain**coat, **i**sn't she?

The **blue rain**coat is **too bright**, **i**sn't it?

Blue suits her, **do**esn't it?

4.2b Say the following sentences, adding a question tag.

She looks terrible in blue,
The brown raincoat is very large,
It's the only one left,
The yellow raincoat is the right size,
Brown is fashionable this year,
The brown and cream raincoats have all been sold,

F U R T H E R P R A C T I C E

/l/ Unit 12:1, 2, 4, 6 pages 58–60   /r/ Unit 12:5, 6 pages 59–60

/l/ leg　/n/ no
/r/ ring

T A S K 1　Distinguish between /l/ and /n/ and /r/

1.1　**Listen, and practise the difference.**

low	no	lip	nip
light	night	life	knife
let	net	Kelly	Kenny
Lee	knee	collect	connect

1.2　**Listen to the words on the cassette.**
Write the words you hear.

1.3　**Listen to the sentences on the cassette.**
For each one, write the word you hear.

1 There are low/no sounds in the background.
2 She lost her life/knife.
3 This light/night seems to be lasting a long time.
4 Mrs Kelly/Kenny would like to speak to you.
5 They've collected/connected the television.

1.4　**Listen, and practise the difference.**

low	no	row	collect	connect	correct
light	night	right	Kelly	Kenny	Kerry
lap	nap	rap, wrap	belly	Benny	berry
lip	nip	rip			

T A S K 2　Say /l/

2a　**Listen to the questions. Match up the questions with the answers.**
Then practise them.

What's your favourite colour?	No, not at all.
What time do you usually get up?	Italian.
Have you ever been to London?	Cycling.
Where do you live?	Only English.
How long have you lived there?	Eight o'clock.
What languages do you speak?	In Love Lane.
Do you like getting up early?	Yellow.
What sort of food do you like best?	Eleven years.
What's your favourite sport?	Yes, lots of times.

PW **2b** **Ask a partner the questions in 2a. Then tell the class about your partner.**

> e.g. Hiroko's favourite colour is blue.
> She usually gets up at seven o'clock. *etc.*

T A S K 3   Say /n/

Listen, and practise this conversation. Notice that the words in *italics* are strongly stressed.

A: We're *nearly* there. I've just seen a signpost. It's only nine miles to Newcastle.
B: I'm glad it's nearly the end of the journey. The engine is making a *terrible* noise.
A: Oh, it *always* makes a noise. I *never* take any notice. Nothing *ever* happens.
B: You mean, nothing has happened *yet*!

T A S K 4   Say /l/ and /n/

4a **Listen, and practise.**

A: I loved my junior school. I used to get there early in the morning, and leave as late as possible in the afternoon. When I was eleven, I went to a new school. I liked it a lot, but not as much as the old school.

B: I didn't like my junior school. I was usually naughty in class. The teachers didn't like me. They were pleased when I left. I was pleased too.

C: I liked some lessons. I was lazy, and I only worked in lessons I liked. I liked languages, and I liked acting in plays. But I didn't like science, so I didn't listen. I was always last in science.

GW **4b** **Say what you felt about your junior school. Try to use phrases from the texts in 4a.**

T A S K 5   Say /r/

Listen, and practise this conversation at a hotel reception desk.

A: Good evening. My name is Bridget Rees. I've got a room reserved.
B: Oh Ms Rees. We thought you were coming tomorrow. We have reserved a room for you tomorrow night.
A: Tomorrow night? But I wrote to you. I made the arrangements by phone. Then I wrote and confirmed the reservation.
B: Don't worry. I'm sure there is a room free tonight. ...... Yes, Room 3 is free. Would you sign the register, and I'll ring for the porter. He'll carry your cases to your room.

T A S K 6   Say /l/ and /n/ and /r/

6a   **Listen, and practise this extract from a radio arts programme.**

ANNOUNCER: The Leeds Opera Company has just produced an opera by the
Italian composer Carino. Carino wrote the opera in 1803, and it
was performed in Rome and London. Then it was lost. It was
only found last year, locked up in a drawer in an old London
library.

Here on the programme tonight is a leading singer from the
Leeds Opera Company, Gillian Reed. Gillian, tell us what the
opera is about.

GILLIAN: It's the story of a rich man, played by the famous tenor Roger
Knight. One night he is alone, and he hears a knock at the
door. The door is closed and locked, but suddenly he sees a girl
inside the room. It is a girl he once loved. He left her because he
wanted to marry a rich woman, and the girl killed herself. Now
her spirit returns. The tenor is terrified.
This is a really frightening moment. The lights are low, and
there is a glow around the spirit. – But I'm not going to tell you
the rest of the story. You'll have to come to Leeds and see the
opera.

6b   **Listen, and practise these questions and answers.**

Did Carino write an opera? Yes, he did. He wrote one in 1803.

Was it performed? Yes, it was. In Rome and London.

PW   **Now ask and answer questions about the opera. Use these points (and
your own ideas):**

lost?   found recently?   in a library?   locked up?   just been produced?

PW   **6c**   **Below are some events from the story of Carino's opera. They are in
the wrong order. With a partner, decide the right order. Tell the story.**

He left the girl.   Her spirit returned to the man.
The man was terrified.   He wanted to marry a rich woman.
The girl killed herself.   A rich man loved a girl.

GW   **6d**   **How do you think the story ends? Discuss in a group, and tell the rest
of the class.**

F U R T H E R   P R A C T I C E

/l/r/ Unit 11 page 55   /n/ Unit 15:1, 3, 4, 6, 7 pages 67–69

/v/ voice /f/ five
/p/ pen

T A S K 1 Distinguish between /v/ and /f/ and /p/

1.1 **Listen, and practise the difference.**

van	fan	leave	leaf
very	ferry	save	safe
veil	fail	alive	a life
veal	feel	believe	belief
vine	fine	prove	proof
vole	foal		

1.2 **Listen to the words on the cassette.**
Write the words you hear.

1.3 **Listen to the sentences on the cassette.**
For each one, write the word you hear.

1 We saw a vole/foal by the river.
2 She bought an expensive van/fan.
3 He had a view/few.
4 The vines/fines are quite high.
5 The USA has vast/fast motorways.

1.4 **Listen, and practise the difference.**

faint	paint	fit	pit
fail	pale	farm	palm
fast	past	feel	peel
foot	put	fat	pat
fray	pray	coffee	copy
fair	pair, pear	fort	port

1.5 **Listen to the words on the cassette.**
Write the words you hear.

1.6 **Listen to the sentences on the cassette.**
For each one, write the word you hear.

1 The notice on the door said 'FULL/PULL'.
2 She enjoyed the fair/pear.
3 They sold their figs/pigs at the market.
4 The fees/peas are very expensive.
5 There's a fan/pan on the table.
6 Colchester was a Roman fort/port.

T A S K 2 Say /v/

Listen, and practise this news story.

This evening, police stopped a van containing seven men. Five of the men were carrying knives. In the van were several very valuable paintings. The driver said a friend gave him the paintings when he had to leave his large house. He couldn't remember where the friend lived. The police didn't believe him. They drove the van to the police station. The seven men are still there.

T A S K 3 Say /f/

Listen, and practise this conversation.

A: It's Philippa's fourth birthday on Friday.
B: That's funny. Philippa is fifteen.
A: Yes, she's fifteen. But it's her fourth birthday. She was born on February 29th. So she only has a birthday every four years.

T A S K 4 Say /v/ and /f/

4a **Listen to two people talking about their lives. Practise what they say.**

A: My father's job involves travelling. We have to move quite often. We've lived in five different places in the last seven years. I love it. I've got friends I can visit in all five places. But my mother hates moving. She hates leaving her friends. She says she leaves part of herself behind, every time she moves.

B: I work in an office in the capital, but live in a village. Well, just outside the village, in fact. In an old farmhouse. I grow flowers and vegetables. I like the fresh air, and the people are very friendly. I love the country. But the travelling is difficult. The traffic is awful. I often leave home before seven, and don't arrive at the office till half past eight.

4b **Discuss your feelings about the following.**

a) moving house frequently
b) living in a city or living in a village
c) living near your work or travelling to work

T A S K 5 Say /f/ and /p/

5.1 **Quiz. In pairs, ask and answer these questions.**

1 Is a dolphin a fish?
2 Are potatoes fruit?
3 Can penguins fly?
4 Do tigers come from Africa?
5 Which country produces most coffee?
6 Who were the first people to fly the Atlantic?
(answers on page 122)

5.2 Listen, and practise this conversation in a group of four. Notice the intonation in the 'Before' – sentences: the voice rises in the first part of the sentence, and falls in the last part.

A: Which is the most useful machine in your office?

B: The personal computer. I can put facts and figures into the computer, and find them again fast. Before we had the computer, I could never find the right piece of paper.

C: The photocopier. I can type a draft, correct it, then make copies on the photocopier. Before we had the photocopier, it was awfully difficult to make perfect copies.

D: The coffee machine. I can have a cup of coffee whenever I feel like it. Before we had the coffee machine, I had to fetch coffee from the café next door.

B: I preferred it when you had to go to the café. Now there are coffee cups all over the office.

C: And yesterday I had just made forty-four perfect copies, and you poured a cup of coffee all over them.

Which of the machines do the following people need?

Frank wants four copies of a paper.   Fred is thirsty.
Felicity wants facts and figures fast.

TASK 6 Say /v/ and /f/ and /p/

Listen to a supervisor in a supermarket. She is telling someone where to put some fruit and vegetables. Listen and label the picture below.

Now describe where the things are.

FURTHER PRACTICE

/v/ Unit 14:1, 3, 5 page 64–66   /p/ Unit 8:1, 2, 4 page 46–48.

U N I T 14 /b/ bad /v/ voice
/w/ wet

T A S K 1 Distinguish between /b/ and /v/ and /w/

1.1 **Listen, and practise the difference.**

best	vest	berry	very
boat	vote	bolts	volts
bowl	vole	ban	van
bat	vat	bet	vet

1.2 **Listen to the words on the cassette.**
Write the words you hear.

1.3 **Listen to the sentences on the cassette.**
For each one, write the word you hear.

1 I haven't got a boat/vote.
2 There's a grey bowl/vole over there.
3 How many bolts/volts are there?
4 I think there's a ban/van.
5 Have you got a bet/vet?

1.4 **Listen, and practise the difference.**

vet	wet	via	wire
vest	west	vine	wine
veil	wail, whale	v	we
verse	worse	veal	wheel

1.5 **Listen to the words on the cassette.**
Write the words you hear.

1.6 **Listen to the sentences on the cassette.**
For each one, write the word you hear.

1 This veal/wheel is no good.
2 The vest/west is over there.
3 The country's vines/wines are famous.
4 You don't see many veils/whales in this area.
5 He never wrote a verse/worse play.

T A S K 2 Say /b/

2a **Listen, and say what happened to this person.**

My brother had a bad time last winter.
In September, his bicycle was stolen.
In October, he lost his job.
In November, his bungalow was burgled.
In December, nobody remembered his birthday.
In February, he broke his elbow.

2b **Test your memory. Cover the sentences in 2a. Can you say what
happened in each month?**

T A S K 3 Say /v/

Listen, and practise this conversation.

A: Good evening. I saw your advertisement about a television for sale. I'm interested in a second-hand television. Is it still available?

B: Yes, it is. It's a lovely television. I've only had it seven months. But I'm moving, and a large television isn't very convenient. Come and have a look. It's over here.

A: Yes, it looks very nice. Your advertisement said £77.

B: Yes, £77, including delivery.

A: I've got a van, so I don't need it delivered. I'll give you £70.

B: OK. You can have it.

T A S K 4 Say /w/

4a Listen, and repeat these statements.

William went for a walk.
William heard something wonderful last week.
Winnie went to work at the same time all week.
Winnie had lunch at a wine bar.
William went away on holiday.
Winnie went out through the window.
William wants wet weather next week.

** **4b** Now make Wh-questions about the statements in 4a. Make sure your voice falls in the questions.

e.g. William went for a walk. (Where ..... ?)

Where did he go?

William heard something wonderful last week. (What ..... ? When ..... ?)
Winnie went to work at the same time all week. (What time ..... ?)
Winnie had lunch at a wine bar. (Which ..... ? When ..... ? What ..... ?)
William went away on holiday. (When ..... ? Where ..... ?)
Winnie went out through the window. (Why ..... ? Which ..... ?
When ..... ?)
William wants wet weather next week. (Why ..... ?)

T A S K 5 Say /b/ and /v/ and /w/

5.1a **Listen, and practise.**

Bob is very worried about his friends. Barbara weighs 70 kilos, and is very unfit. Ben has a violent temper, and he's always in trouble. Vera's job is boring, and she always feels tired. And he never sees Wendy because she is so busy.

5.1b **Match the names and the descriptions below.**

e.g. Bob's very worried.

Bob   Barbara   Ben   Vera   Wendy

overweight   bored and weary   very worried   always violent
very busy

5.2a **Listen, and practise this conversation.**

A: What can I give my brother for his birthday?
B: What does he do for a living?
A: He's a van driver.
B: Give him some driving gloves.
A: He doesn't wear gloves when he drives, not even in winter.
B: What does he do as a hobby?
A: In warm weather, he goes swimming. And he plays golf.
B: Give him some golf clubs.
A: He's already got a bag full of golf clubs. His golf bag is so heavy he can hardly move it.
A: What does he do in the winter?
B: He belongs to a football club. But he spends more time drinking beer in the bar than playing football.
A: That solves your problem. Give him a big bottle of beer!

5.2b **Look at the list of presents below. Which things would be good presents for A's brother. Explain why, or why not.**

driving gloves   golf clubs   a golf bag   a football   a bottle of beer
a bottle of wine   a book about vegetables   a record of violin music
a watch   a whistle   a beach ball   swimming trunks

5.2c **Discuss what presents to give to other students, or your family or friends. Choose from the list in 5.2b, or think of other things with /b/, /v/, or /w/.**

e.g. My friend Brenda swims very well. I would give her a bikini.

F U R T H E R   P R A C T I C E

/b/ Unit 8:1, 3, 4 pages 46–48   /v/ Unit 13:1, 2, 4, 6 pages 61–63

UNIT 15

/n/ no, pin
/ŋ/ thing
/m/ me, thumb

T A S K 1 Distinguish between /n/ and /ŋ/

1.1 Listen, and practise the difference.

sin	sing	sinner	singer
ran	rang	win	wing
ton	tongue	thin	thing
son, sun	sung	ban	bang

**1.2 Listen to the words on the cassette.
Write the words you hear.**

**1.3 Listen to the sentences on the cassette.
For each one, write the word you hear.**

1 Stop sinning/singing.
2 He ran/rang home.
3 I think they will ban/bang it.
4 She's a terrible sinner/singer.

T A S K 2 Say /m/

Listen, and practise this conversation.

A: We must make sure the front bedroom is warm.
B: Why?
A: Don't you remember? My mother and father are coming tomorrow.
B: What time?
A: I'm going to meet them at the airport at four. Can you come?
B: No, I won't be home from work in time. But I'll be home in time to say
'Welcome'.

T A S K 3 Say /n/

Listen, and practise this extract from the radio news.

Here is the weather forecast for today, the ninth of November.

In the north, there will be rain and snow in the morning.
In the afternoon there will be sunny intervals. Central districts
will have rain and snow showers, with a little sun. The south
will have sunny intervals and occasional rain. Tomorrow,
there will be rain again, but the next day we shall have more sun.

And now here are the main points of the news again .....

T A S K 4 Say /m/ and /n/

4a **Listen, and practise this conversation.**

A: I want to watch television at ten to seven.
B: What's on?
A: An American programme, about a family on a farm.
B: Is that the programme where the mother got married again?
A: Yes, and the son ran away from home last summer. His mother imagined he came home again, but it was only a dream.
B: Well, I want to watch the nine o'clock news.
A: OK. No problem. My programme ends at half past seven.

4b **Listen, and practise correcting incorrect statements. Notice how the voice falls to emphasise the correct information.**

The **television programme** be**gins** at **ten** to **nine**.

No, the **television programme** be**gins** at **ten** to s**ven**.

It is an Aust**ral**ian **programme**.

No, it is an Am**er**ican **programme**.

PW

Now correct these statements.

**

The programme is about animals on a farm.
The father got married again.
The son ran away from school.
He ran away last autumn.
He came home again.
The programme ends at twenty past seven.
B wants to watch *News at Ten*.

T A S K 5 Say /ŋ/

Listen, and practise this conversation from a TV programme.

A: Good evening. My guest tonight is the young singer, Kay King.
B: Good evening.
A: Kay, what were you doing earlier today?
B: I was recording a song called 'Bells are Ringing'.
A: Did the recording go well?
B: Yes. Sometimes everything goes wrong, but today nothing went wrong. I think 'Bells are Ringing' is going to be the top song, this spring.

TASK 6 Say /n/ and /ŋ/

6.1 Listen, and practise this television announcement.

Britain has won the European Golden Song Contest, for the ninth time. The winning song is 'Bells are Ringing', sung by Kay King. Last year's winners, Sweden, came second. Their new song is called 'Bing Bang Bong'. Runners-up were Denmark, with the song 'It's Spring Again, I'm Young Again'.

6.2 Listen, and practise this conversation.

A: We're feeling anxious.
B: We're feeling angry.
A: We didn't sleep last night. The gate was banging all night.
B: And the children from next door keep ringing the doorbell and running away.
A: And the telephone keeps ringing.
B: And when we answer it, it's a wrong number.
A: And now the television has gone wrong.
B: That's why we're feeling angry.
A: And anxious.

TASK 7 Say /m/ and /n/ and /ŋ/

Fill in this questionnaire from a magazine. Then ask two other people, and fill in their answers.

KNOW YOURSELF – Which of these things make you anxious?			
	You		
Answering the telephone			
Getting a wrong number			
Getting up late in the morning			
Not knowing the time			
Learning English			
Listening to English songs			
Coming home alone			
Going shopping			
Watching the news on television			

FURTHER PRACTICE

/n/ Unit 12:3, 4, 6 pages 59–60

UNIT 16

/θ/ thin /s/ so
/ð/ this /z/ zoo

TASK 1 Distinguish between /θ/, /s/, /ð/ and /z/

1.1 Listen, and practise the difference.

thick	sick	path	pass
think	sink	mouth	mouse
theme	seem	moth	moss
thumb	sum	worth	worse
thing	sing	tenth	tense

**1.2 Listen to the words on the cassette.
Write the words you hear.**

**1.3 Listen to the sentences on the cassette.
For each one, write the word you hear.**

1 Be careful! He's thinking/sinking.
2 What's the matter? Your thumb/sum doesn't look right.
3 There's a path/pass high up in the mountains.
4 Every mouth/mouse is different.
5 That moth/moss was shown in a television programme.

1.4 Listen, and practise the difference.

breathe	breeze	then	Zen
teething	teasing	though	zone
clothing	closing	this	zip
bathe	bays	these	zero

**1.5 Listen to the words on the cassette.
Write the words you hear.**

TASK 2 Say /θ/

Quiz. In pairs, make questions and answers. e.g.

1 Would you wear a thimble on your finger or thumb?

2 North Pole or South Pole?

3 Eat it or throw it?

4 3rd or 4th month?

5 Healthy or unhealthy?

39

TASK 3 Say /θ/ and /s/

3a   Listen, and practise this conversation.

A: I think there's something wrong with me.
B: What's the matter?
A: I've got a sore throat.
B: That doesn't sound very serious.
A: My throat has been sore for three days. And I'm thirsty.
B: Well the weather is hot. I expect that's why you feel thirsty.
A: You're not very sympathetic. I'm thinking of going to the Health Centre. If there's anything seriously wrong with my throat, Doctor Thorne will see to me.
B: I don't think it's worth it. Doctor Thorne will be less sympathetic than me.

3b   Listen, and practise correcting incorrect statements. Notice how the voice falls to emphasise the correct word.

A has a **sore thumb**.   No, A has a **sore throat**.

B is **very sympathetic**.   No, B isn't **very sympathetic**.

Now correct the following incorrect statements.

His thumb has been sore for three days.
He feels hungry.
The weather is thundery.
A is thinking of going to the swimming bath.
B thinks Doctor Thorne will be sympathetic.

TASK 4 Say /ð/

Listen, and practise this conversation.

A: Good morning, Mr Motherwell. What can I do for you this morning?
B: Good morning, Doctor Wetherley. It's my breathing. I get this pain when I breathe in.
A: I'll listen to your chest. Breathe in, and breathe out. And again, breathe in, and breathe out. Keep breathing deeply.
B: Is there anything wrong with my chest, doctor?
A: No, I don't think so. Your breathing sounds fine. Have you got a pillow with feathers in it?
B: No.
A: Or any leather clothes?
B: I've got a new leather jacket.
A: That may be the problem. Leather affects some people like that. Get rid of your leather jacket, and I think that pain will go.

T A S K 5 Say /ð/ and /z/

5.1   **These are some photographs of Susan and Jonathan's wedding.**

Some of their friends are talking about the photographs. Listen, and repeat what they say.

That's his father.	His brother is very handsome.
It was nice weather.	His mother's carrying roses.
That's her brother.	She always wears beautiful clothes.
She's got two brothers.	They seem to be enjoying
That's the other brother	themselves.
over there.	

5.2a   Listen and repeat the sentence below. The speaker is certain of what she says. She expects the others to agree with her. Her voice falls on the question tag.

His **bro**ther is very **ha**ndsome, **i**sn't he?

5.2b   Listen and repeat the sentence below. Here, the speaker is not certain. He is asking for confirmation. His voice rises on the question tag.

That's his **fa**ther, **i**sn't it?

5.2c   Listen to the speakers on the cassette. They are saying the statements in 5.1, with question tags. For each one, decide whether the speaker is certain, or not certain.

5.3   Say the statements in 5.1, adding a question tag. For each one, choose whether you are certain or not certain. Your partner must decide whether you are certain or not certain.

FURTHER PRACTICE

/θ/ð/ Unit 17 page 73; Unit 18 page 76
/s/ Unit 2:1, 2, 4 pages 28–30; Unit 6:1, 2, 4 page 40, 42
/z/ Unit 6:1, 3, 4 pages 40–42

TASK 1 Distinguish between /θ/, /t/, /ð/ and /d/

1.1 Listen, and practise the difference.

thin	tin	heath	heat
thank	tank	sheath	sheet
thick	tick	fourth	fort
three	tree	path	part
theme	team	north	nought

1.2 Listen to the words on the cassette.
Write the words you hear.

1.3 Listen to the sentences on the cassette.
For each one, write the word you hear.

1 I never knew what she thought/taught.
2 The theme/team was very popular.
3 We kept it in a thin/tin box.
4 Which path/part are you going to take?
5 I don't like the heath/heat.

1.4 Listen, and practise the difference.

there	dare	breathe	breed
then	den	worthy	wordy
than	Dan	lather	ladder
though	dough		

1.5 Listen to the words on the cassette.
Write the words you hear.

TASK 2 Say /θ/ and /t/

Listen, and practise this conversation.

A: You forgot Theo's birthday on Tuesday!
B: Oh no! I knew his birthday was this month, but I thought it was the tenth.
A: No, it's the fourth.
B: Did he have a birthday party?
A: Yes, he had thirteen friends to tea.
B: Goodness! I didn't think three-year-olds had as many as thirteen friends.

T A S K 3   Say /d/ at the end of words

3.1   **Listen, and say these adjectives ending in /ə/.**

afraid   bad   boiled   good   hard   loud   old   red

Now use them to fill the gaps in these phrases

a ___*bad*___ accident   _____white and blue

an ___*Good*___ friend   a ___*red*___ apple

a ___*bad*___ friend   ___*afraid*___ of the dark.

a _____ explosion   a ___*boiled*___ egg

3.2   **Listen, and say these nouns ending in /d/.**

bed   side   Head   end

Now use them to fill the gaps in these phrases.

the _____ of the line   the _____ of Department

the _____ of the road   _____and breakfast

T A S K 4   Say /d/ and /ð/

4a   **Listen to someone talking about their childhood. In the text below, circle the words with /d/ and underline the words with /ð/. The first three are done for you. Then practise the text.**

One (day) when I was in the (third) class, we had to write a story. I told a true story about my father. He wanted to clean the windows. He borrowed a ladder. He tried to put it against the wall, but the end of the ladder went through the window. My teacher said it was a very good story. I had to read it aloud to the other students.

   Three years later, my brother was in that class. He wrote the same story, about my father and the ladder. *He* had to read it aloud, too.

4b   **Listen to these sentences. Notice how the voice rises at the end of the non-final phrases.**

One day, when I was in the third class, we had to write a story.

Three years later, my brother was in that class.

4c   **Make up your own sentences, beginning with the following phrases, or others. Make sure your voice rises at the end of the phrase.**

Yesterday,   Three days ago,   When my father was a boy,
The other day,   Early this morning,   When I was three years old,

T A S K 5 Say /θ/ and /ð/

5.1 Listen, and practise.

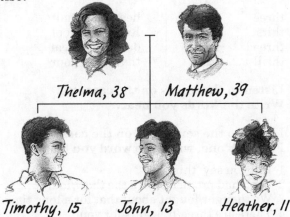

THE
BLYTHE
FAMILY

Thelma, 38   Matthew, 39

Timothy, 15   John, 13   Heather, 11

John Blythe is thirteen. His brother Timothy is fifteen. Their sister Heather is eleven. Their mother and father come from Northern Ireland, but the children were all born in London. Their mother is called Thelma and she is 38. Their father's name is Matthew, and he is 39.

5.2a Listen to Judith Smith on the cassette. Look at her family tree, below. Write in the names and ages of the people in her family.

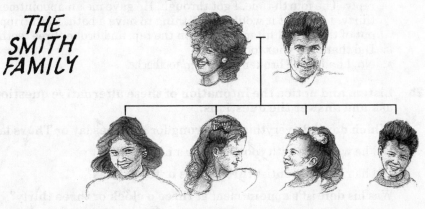

THE
SMITH
FAMILY

5.2b Make true sentences about Judith and her family.

5.3 Describe your family (brothers, sisters, mother, father), or a family you know.

FURTHER PRACTICE

/θ/ð/ Unit 16 page 70; Unit 18 page 76   /t/d/ Unit 9 page 49

U N I T 18

/θ/ thin /f/ fine
/ð/ this /v/ voice

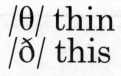

T A S K 1 Distinguish between /θ/ and /f/

1.1 **Listen, and practise the difference.**

three	free	hearth	half
thirst	first	Ruth	roof
thread	Fred	death	deaf
thrill	frill	thaw	four

1.2 **Listen to the words on the cassette.**
Write the words you hear.

1.3 **Listen to the sentences on the cassette.**
For each one, write the word you hear.

1 Did you say 'thin'/'fin'?
2 They had problems with the thaw/four.
3 We thought/fought about that for a long time.
4 There are three/free gifts for you.

T A S K 2 Say /θ/

2a **Listen, and practise this conversation.**

A: Everything went wrong on Thursday.
B: What happened?
A: I woke up with toothache. I rang the dentist three times, but there was no reply. The fourth time, I got through. He gave me an appointment at three thirty. I thought it would be soothing to have a bath. But I tripped getting out of the bath. I hit my mouth on the tap, and broke three teeth.
B: Did that cure your toothache?
A: No, I had three broken teeth *and* toothache.

2b **Listen, and notice the intonation of these alternative questions. Then ask and answer the questions.**

Which day did everything **go wrong** for **A** – **Tues**day or **Thurs**day?

Did he **wake up** with **tooth**ache or a **head**ache?

Did he **ring** the **dentist three** times or **four times**?

Was his **dentist's** ap**point**ment at **three o'clock** or **three thirty**?

When he tripped, did he **break both legs** or **three teeth**?

T A S K 3   Say /θ/ and /f/

3a   **Listen, and read out this extract from a holiday brochure.**

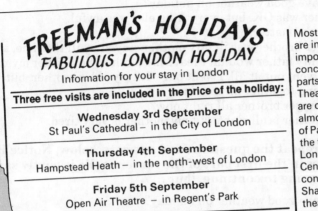

FREEMAN'S HOLIDAYS
FABULOUS LONDON HOLIDAY
Information for your stay in London

Three free visits are included in the price of the holiday:

Wednesday 3rd September
St Paul's Cathedral – in the City of London

Thursday 4th September
Hampstead Heath – in the north-west of London

Friday 5th September
Open Air Theatre – in Regent's Park

Most theatres and cinemas are in the West End. A few important theatres and concert halls are in other parts of London. The National Theatre and the Festival Hall are on the South Bank, almost opposite the Houses of Parliament. In the City, the financial centre of London, there is the Barbican Centre. This includes a fine concert hall, and the Royal Shakespeare Company's theatre.

3b   **Use the information in the brochure above to identify the places marked 1 to 6 on the map below.**

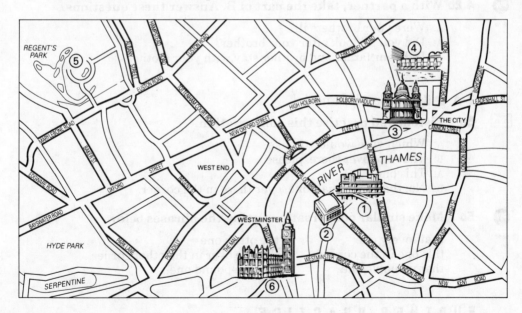

T A S K 4 Say /ð/

4.1 Listen, and practise this conversation.

A: Did you have good weather on holiday?
B: The weather was OK, but everything else was awful.
A: What was the matter?
B: My younger brother was ill. My mother stayed in all the time, to look after him. My father wouldn't leave my mother. So neither my mother nor my father went out at all. I went out with my elder brother, but we got tired of being together all the time.
A: Is your younger brother all right now?
B: Yes, my brother is all right, but my mother is very tired.

4.2a Listen, and repeat the questions and answers below. Notice B's voice falls and rises in the first part of the sentence. He is partly saying 'Yes', but is going to continue, 'but ......'

A: Did you have good weather on holiday?

B: The **weather was OK**, but everything **else** was **awful**.

A: Is your younger brother all right now?

B: **Yes**, my **brother is all right**, but my **mother** is **very tired**.

4.2b With a partner, take the part of B. Answer these questions.

**

A: Were your brothers ill?
A: Did you all look after your brother?
A: Did your father and brother stay with your mother?

T A S K 5 Say /ð/ and /v/

5a Listen, and practise this conversation.

A: Which vase would you like?
B: That one over there, please.
A: This one?
B: No, that very small one, over there in the corner.

5b Make similar conversations using the phrases below.

**

that lovely one   the other one
this one in the corner   the one over in the other corner
that valuable one   the five-pound one

F U R T H E R P R A C T I C E

/θ/ð/ Unit 16 page 70; Unit 17 page 73   /v/f/ Unit 13 page 61
/v/ Unit 14:1, 3, 5 pages 64–66

Consonant clusters 1 – beginning of words

TASK 1   Say clusters with /p, b, t, d, k, g/ followed by /w, r, l, j/

1.1   Listen, and repeat.

A: The train for Bladon leaves from Platform 1.
B: Meet me under the clock.

Now make similar conversations about these places.

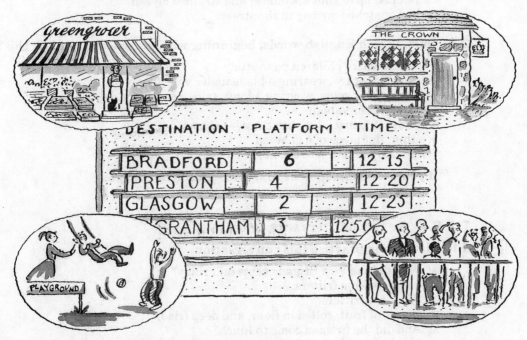

1.2a Listen, and practise this conversation.

A: Excuse me, is this the Bladon train?
B: No, I'm afraid you've just missed the Bladon train. It went at 12.03.
A: But it's only twelve o'clock now. Look at the clock.
B: No, that clock's three minutes slow.

1.2b Make similar conversations about the trains shown in 1.1.

[○○]   **1.3   Listen, and practise these conversations.**

    A: I've got a job with the BBC.
    B: The British Broadcasting Corporation?
    A: No, the Brighton Brush Company.

    A: I didn't sleep very well last night.
    B: Was your brain full of brilliant ideas?
    A: No, there were breadcrumbs in the blankets.

T A S K 2   Say clusters beginning with /s/

[○○]   **2.1   Listen, and practise describing these problems.**

I was stung on the wrist by a wasp. I screamed.
I slipped down the steps and sprained my ankle.
We had a puncture, and our spare wheel was flat.
I stretched up to shut a window, and strained myself.
A thief snatched my bag in the street.

2.2   Quiz. Which English words, beginning with 's', are defined like this?

    1 a place where children go to study
    2 to slide over ice, wearing a blade under your foot
    3 to slide over snow, wearing a long strip of metal under your foot
    4 frozen water vapour
    5 to rest, unconscious, with the eyes closed
    6 a thin, flat piece of e.g. bread
    7 a country situated to the north of England

If you need help, look at the words on the next page.

T A S K 3   Say clusters with /f, θ, ʃ/

[○○]   **3.1   Listen, and practise this conversation.**

    A: Why did the Fire Brigade come on Friday?
    B: I was cooking fritters.
    A: What are fritters?
    B: Pieces of fruit, rolled in flour, and deep fried.
    A: And did the firemen come to lunch?
    B: No. As I was frying the fritters, suddenly there was a flash, and flames
        from the frying pan. So I shrieked, and threw the fritters on the floor, and
        rang for the Fire Brigade.

3.2   **Listen, and practise this conversation.**

A: Splendid cricket match!
B: Who won?
A: We did! Shropshire needed three runs to win. Shrimpton hit the ball. Fletcher tried to catch it, but it slipped through his fingers.
B: Oh no! So Shrimpton got his three runs, I suppose.
A: No, Thrush was just behind Fletcher. He flung himself forward .....
B: And he caught the ball?
A: No, but he picked it up, and threw it, and Shrimpton was out!
B: What a thrilling ending!

T A S K 4   Say clusters

4a   **Listen, and practise this conversation.**

A: What are you doing on Tuesday?
B: I'm going to a play by J B Priestley.
A: What's it called?
B: 'An Inspector Calls'.

4b   **Make similar conversations about the arrangements in the diary.**

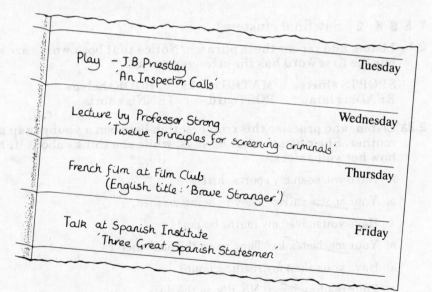

Play – J.B. Prestley
'An Inspector Calls'   Tuesday

Lecture by Professor Strong   Wednesday
'Twelve principles for screening criminals'

French film at Film Club   Thursday
(English title : 'Brave Stranger')

Talk at Spanish Institute   Friday
'Three Great Spanish Statesmen'

Words for the Quiz in 2.2. Match each word with the correct definition. Practise saying them. Listen to the cassette to check.

snow   school   skate   slice   Scotland   ski   sleep

Consonant clusters 2
– end and
middle of words

TASK 1 Say past tenses

1a **Listen, and repeat these verbs.**

1 dragged   escaped   grabbed   locked   opened   robbed
  rushed   unlocked
2 cracked   dropped   helped   jumped   knocked   smashed
  wiped

1b **Use the verbs to fill the gaps in the stories below. Practise them.
Listen to the cassette to check.**

1 Three masked men _____ the City Bank yesterday. When the
  doors were _____, they _____ in. They _____
  the manager, and _____ him into the strongroom. They
  _____ the safe with his keys. Then they _____ the
  manager in, and _____ with £30,000.

2 When I _____ at the door, he _____, and
  _____ three eggs on the floor. Of course, they _____.
  I _____ him as he _____ up the mess. His glasses fell
  on the floor. The glass _____.

TASK 2 Say final clusters

2.1 **Listen, and repeat these phrases. Notice that both words are stressed,
but the first word has the stronger stress.**

SPORTS shirts   MATHS books   BOOKshelves
READing lamp   POSTcards   TENNis shorts

2.2a **Listen, and practise this conversation between a young man and his
mother. She repeats what he says, while she thinks about it. Notice
how her voice rises.**

A: Have you seen my sports shirts?

B: Your sports shirts? They're being washed.

A: Have you moved my maths books?

B: Your maths books? They're on the bookshelves.

A: Have you taken my reading lamp?

B: Your reading lamp? No, it's on the desk.

A: Can I borrow some postcards?

B: Postcards? All right. They're in the drawer, with the envelopes.

A: Will you iron my tennis shorts?

B: Your tennis shorts? No, you can iron them yourself!

2.2b Practise the conversation again. This time, don't look at the text. The pictures below will remind you what A is looking for.

T A S K 3 Say /t/ or /d/ followed by /n/

3a Listen, and practise this conversation in a department store. Notice the intonation of A's polite phrases.

A: Excuse me, I'm looking for some sewing cotton.
B: Pardon?
A: I'm looking for some sewing cotton. Can you tell me which department I need?
B: I'm not certain.
A: Well, is it Fashion or Haberdashery?
B: I don't know. You'd better ask an assistant.
A: I beg your pardon. I thought you **were** an assistant.

3b Make similar conversations, using the Store Directory below. Ask for these things.

curtains   wooden bowls   garden furniture   buttons

Ground floor	Basement
Fashion	Kitchenware
Haberdashery	Furniture
Soft Furnishing	Garden Equipment

T A S K 4 Say /t, d/ or /n/ followed by /l/

4a Listen and read out this notice.

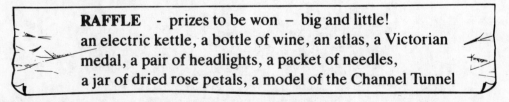

RAFFLE - prizes to be won – big and little!
an electric kettle, a bottle of wine, an atlas, a Victorian
medal, a pair of headlights, a packet of needles,
a jar of dried rose petals, a model of the Channel Tunnel

4b Which things would you like to win? Which would you not like? List them in order of preference. Read out your list.

T A S K 5 Say clusters

5a **Listen, and practise these instructions for Keep Fit exercises.**

Stand with your back straight, and feet a little way apart. Your toes should be pointing to the front. Swing your arms up. Keep them straight. Stretch up, with your hands high up above your head. And relax.

Put the backs of your hands on your ribs, just above the waist. Feel your ribs move outwards as you breathe in. Take a deep breath, hold it, and breathe out.

Put your hands by your sides. Circle your head. This helps to relax the neck. Put your head down in front. Turn it to the right. Now let your head drop back. And round to the left. And in front again.

Put your hands on your hips. Bend to the side – first left then right. And rest!

5b **In groups, one student reads out the instructions. The others do the exercises!**

T A S K 6 Say longer clusters of consonants

6a **Listen, and practise.**

Last Sunday, I had a strange dream. I was walking up a long street. I came into a small square, with a fountain. There was a big church. A bride was standing outside, in a beautiful wedding dress. Suddenly there was a loud cry from a tall building opposite. The bridegroom was looking out of a window on the fifth floor. He jumped into the fountain, with a big splash. Then I woke up.

6b **Listen, and repeat these false statements about the dream in 6a.**

She was walking over a wide bridge.
She came into a small street.
A bride was standing outside a small cottage.
There was a loud cry from the church.
The bridegroom was on the roof of the tall building.
He jumped through the window of the big church.

Now say each of the statements correctly. Use stress and intonation to emphasise the correct facts.

This unit will help you to link words together smoothly. Think of the words joined together like this: Putitaway.
Or imagine that the last letter of a word is the first letter of the next
word: a big apple — a bi gapple
          read a book — rea da book
In this unit, words to link are shown like this: put it away, read it

T A S K 1   Link /p, b, t, d, k, g/ to a following vowel

1a   **Listen to people giving advice. Practise it.**

My neck aches.

> Wrap it in a scarf.
>
> Drink a cup of tea
>
> Take an aspirin.
>
> Don't think about it.
>
> Rub it.

I've got a big emerald ring.

> Put it on.
>
> Keep it safe.
>
> Lock it up.
>
> Take it to the bank.
>
> Put it in a big envelope, and hide it under the bed.

I've got a week off. What shall I do?

> Make a dress.
>
> Knit a jumper.
>
> Read a book.
>
> Paint a picture.
>
> Sit and relax.

What would Anne like for Christmas?

> a big umbrella
>
> a bag and some gloves
>
> a book on music
>
> a red and white scarf

1b   **What would *you* advise? Discuss with other students.**

T A S K 2   Link /f, v, ∫, t∫, dʒ, s, z, θ/ to a following vowel

Listen, and practise this conversation.

A: What do you want to do when you leave school?
B: I want to move into a flat with some friends.
A: It's less expensive to live at home.
B: I'm going to give a party.
A: Don't damage anything!
B: I'd like to buy myself a sports car.
A: Don't crash into anything!
B: I want to catch a plane to South America.
A: Arrange a cheap flight!
B: What do you want to do when you leave school?
A: I want to get a job in a large organisation, and save all my money.

T A S K 3   Link /r/ to a following vowel

Listen to this conversation in a hospital waiting room. Note that you can pronounce /r/ at the end of a word, when the next word begins with a vowel. Mark the links in A's last speech.

A: We've been waiting for an hour and a half.
B: Say your aunt is very ill. A doctor ought to see her at once.
A: There isn't a doctor available. They're all busy.
B: Ask the receptionist to hurry up.
A: I've asked her over and over again. The more I ask, the longer I wait.

Now practise the conversation.

T A S K 4   Link vowels /iː, ɪ, aɪ, eɪ, ɔɪ/ to a following vowel

Listen, and repeat. Think of a little / j / sound (as in 'yes' / jes /) linking two words. Mark the links in the last group.

very ʲ interesting
the story ʲ is very ʲ interesting.
The ʲ end of the story ʲ is very ʲ interesting.
a lovely ʲ ice cream
enjoy ʲ a lovely ʲ ice cream.
I ʲ always enjoy ʲ a lovely ʲ ice cream.
a day or two
stay at home for a day or two
I ought to stay at home for a day or two.

T A S K 5 Link vowels /uː, əʊ, aʊ/ to a following vowel

5a **Listen, and repeat these sentences which were all overheard at a party. Think of a little /w/ sound linking two words. Mark the links in the last four sentences.**

I couldn't do ͜ʷ anything about it.

Let's go ͜ʷ into the next room.

Do you know ͜ʷ everyone here?

I've moved to a new ͜ʷ office – next to ͜ʷ Oxford Circus station.

I knew ͜ʷ I would be late.

Are you ͜ʷ in the same place?

You ͜ʷ always say that.

It was so ͜ʷ exciting.

I don't know ͜ʷ all the students, but I know ͜ʷ all the teachers.

How old is he?

There was snow and ice everywhere.

We travelled through Africa.

I don't know anything about him.

5b **Discuss which of the sentences above might have come from the same conversations.**

T A S K 6 Recognise and produce links with all sounds

Listen to this conversation which contains words ending with each of the consonants practised in this unit, followed by a vowel, and also of linking with ʳ, ʲ and ʷ. Look for an example of each type of link and mark the link.

A: Anne's just phoned. She and Diana are both on their way. Is dinner nearly ready? Can I help with anything?

B: Yes. Can you get out two eggs from the fridge?

A: Which eggs? The large ones or the small ones?

B: The large eggs. Small eggs are no good.

A: OK. Anything else?

B: Yes. Squeeze another orange, and put the fresh orange juice in a jug, please.

A: Right. What next?

B: There's a pie in the oven. Take it out, and slide it under the grill. Then finish laying the table for me. Each person needs a knife and fork, and a cup and saucer. And then, could you scrub all these potatoes.

A: Come on, Anne and Diana!

Now practise the conversation, linking the words smoothly.

Some words and syllables are pronounced more strongly than others: they are **stressed**. (In this unit, stressed syllables are marked in **bold** type.) In unstressed words and syllables, the sound /ə/ is often used.

T A S K 1 Say /ə/ in unstressed syllables

1.1a Listen, and repeat. Make the stressed syllables strong, and the unstressed syllables weak and quick.

> **Try** a**gain**.   **Come** a**long**.
> **Paul**'s a **post**man.   **Mar**tha's a **teach**er.
> **Mich**ael's a po**lice**man.   **Bar**bara's a **pi**lot.
> A **col**oured **pic**ture.

In all the unstressed syllables above, the sound /ə/ is used. Notice that /ə/ can be spelled in many ways.

1.1b Look again at the phrases in 1.1a. Find words where /ə/ is spelled a, e, o, u.

1.2 Listen to these phrases, and mark the stressed syllables. Then practise the phrases; be careful to use /ə/ in the unstressed syllables.

> Go away.   Come again.
> Susan's a singer.   Jill's a photographer.
> John and Michael are policemen.   Brian's a bus conductor.
> A big adventure.

T A S K 2 Say /ə/ in weak forms

Many common words have a weak form, with / ə /, when unstressed:

2.1 'and'   The following words often appear in a phrase with 'and'. For each word, say a phrase.

> e.g. **knife** and **fork**

> 1 knife   2 black   3 ladies   4 fish   5 bacon   6 here   7 up

> **Now listen to the phrases on the cassette to check. Can you think of some more phrases with 'and'?**

2.2 'to'   Listen, and repeat.

> 11.50   'It's **ten** to **twelve**.'   3.45   'It's **quarter** to **four**.'

Now say the times shown below.

2.3a 'than'   Compare the people shown below. How many true things can you say?

e.g. **Cath**erine is **taller** than **Sus**an.

Catherine, 22 yrs,   Susan, 24 yrs,   Alan, 20 yrs,   Brian, 28 yrs,
175 cm, 63 kilos   160 cm, 70 kilos   163 cm, 60 kilos   183 cm, 90 kilos

2.3b Make similar sentences about people in your class, or in your family.

2.4a 'of'   Listen, and repeat.

a **bott**le of **wine**   a **cup** of **tea**   a **glass** of **wine**,
a **bag** of potatoes   a **tin** of **beans**   a **pack**et of **sweets**
a **box** of **choc**olates   a **jug** of **water**

2.4b Make similar phrases using these words.

beer   sugar   coffee   matches   tomatoes   milk   chocolate

2.5a 'can'   Listen, and repeat.

I can **swim** quite **well.**
I can **speak French** and **Ger**man.
I can **swim** but I **can't play ten**nis.

(PW) **2.5b** **In pairs, say which of these things you can do.**

> type   speak Chinese/German/French, etc.   play chess
> play tennis/football, etc.   play the guitar/piano, etc.
> drive   ride a bicycle   ride a horse   ski   cook
> (think of other things too)

2.5c **Tell other students about your partner.**

> e.g. **Jean** can **speak French** and **German.**
> **Maria** can **swim very well** but she **can't play ten**nis.

T A S K 3 Say /ə/ in weak forms and unstressed syllables

3.1 **Listen, and notice the words with the sound /ə/ marked in *italics*. Practise the conversation.**

> A: **What** *shall* we **have** *for* **supper?**
> B: **Would** you **like ba**con *and* **eggs?**
> A: **No, not ba**con *and* **eggs tonight. What else** *have* we **got?**
> B: There *are some* **potatoes,** *and* **lots** *of* **tomatoes. We could** have **baked potatoes,** *and a* **tomato salad.**
> A: I **had** *a* **baked potato yesterday.**
> B: **Well** then, you *can* **buy** *some* **fish** *and* **chips,** *from the* **shop** *at* the **end** *of the* **road.**
> A: **OK. Shall** we **have** *a* **bottle** *of* **wine?**
> B: **No, just** *a* **jug** *of* **water.**

3.2 **Listen, and notice the words with the sound /ə/ marked in *italics*. Mark other words which contain the sound /ə/.**

> A: **My sister** is **coming** *to* **see** me **tomorrow.** I'd **like** *to* **take** *her to the* **theatre.** I **wonder what's on.**
> B: **Look** in *the* **news**paper. In *the* **section** called **Entertainments.**
> A: **Oh, yes. Look,** *at the* **Players Theatre. There's** *a* **comedy,** with **Amanda Morgan,** *and* **Michael Allen.**
> B: I've **heard** *of* **Amanda Morgan,** but **who's Michael Allen?**
> A: He **was in** that **television series** *about* a **hospital.** He **played** the **doctor** who **came** from **Canada.**
> B: **Oh yes,** I **remember. Tomorrow** is a **good night** to **go** to the **theatre. On Mon**days, you can get **two seats** for the **price** *of* **one.**
> A: **That's good. Usually,** when I **go** to the **theatre,** I **sit** at the **back.** It's **not** as **comfortable,** but it's **cheaper.** But **tomorrow** we can af**ford better seats,** at the **front.**

Now practise the conversation.

TASK 1 Distinguish between /i:/ and /ɪ/

1.1 Listen, and practise the difference.

green	grin	feet	fit
bead	bid	cheek	chick
reason	risen	deep	dip
meal	mill	each	itch

1.2 Listen to the words on the cassette.
Write the words you hear.

1.3 Listen to the sentences on the cassette.
For each one, write the word you hear.

1 The beans/bins were quite cheap.
2 I'm going to leave/live with my brother.
3 Did you feel/fill it?
4 The peach/pitch was bad.
5 He beat/bit the dog.
6 The children were badly beaten/bitten.

TASK 2 Say /i:/

2.1 Listen, and read out these notices.

SPELLING

/i:/ see

Common:
ALL **ee** sleep
MOST **ea** read, eat
e ('*long* e')
be,
these

Less common:
i machine,
police
ie field, piece
ei receive
ey key

NOTE:
ei *comes in the middle of words. At the end of words the spelling is* **ey**.

SPELLING RULE:
i *before* e
except after c

Exception:
people

/ɪ/ if

See page 22.

2.2a Listen, and practise this conversation in a shop.

A: Have you got any cream cheese?
B: Yes, how much cheese do you need?
A: 250 grams please. I'm going to make a cheesecake.

2.2b Make similar conversations with details from these recipes.

Coffee ice cream

Ingredients:
¼ litre cream
1 teaspoon coffee essence

Bean salad

Ingredients:
3 lb green beans
1 sweet red pepper

Peach pie

Ingredients:
6 peaches
100 gm margarine

Pea soup

Ingredients:
2 lb peas
1 small leek

T A S K 3   Say /ɪ/

3.1a Listen, and practise this conversation at a station.

A: Excuse me, when's the next train to Liverpool?
B: Six fifty.
A: Which platform?
B: Platform six.

3.1b Make similar conversations with details from this notice.

DESTINATION	TIME	PLATFORM
BRISTOL	6.15	16
HITCHIN	6.50	6
ILMINSTER	7.50	15
WINCHESTER	10.50	6

3.2a **Listen, and practise this message for a doctor.**

Hello, my name is Gillian Timpson. Please tell Dr Phillips that my daughter
Nicola is ill. She's got little red spots, which itch terribly. And she's got a
high temperature. If she drinks anything, she's sick. I think she needs a
home visit. Our address is 56 Hill Road.

3.2b **The receptionist who took the message told Dr Phillips some wrong
things. Listen, and repeat each one.**

Mrs Simpson called.   She won't drink anything.
Her son Nicolas is ill.   She needs to go to hospital.
She's got big red spots.   They live at 66 Mill Road.

3.2c **Correct the wrong messages. Make sure your voice falls to emphasise
the correct information.**

e.g. A: Mrs Simpson called. B: No, Mrs Timpson called.

T A S K 4 Say /iː/ and /ɪ/

4.1 **Listen, and practise this conversation between two doctors.**

A: Have you been busy this evening?
B: Pretty busy. My first patient was Jim Beaton. He had twisted his knee. He
slipped on a banana skin in the street. I think he just needs to rest his
knee. He's very fit.
A: My first patient was Mrs Neale. She keeps being sick, and it's just
because she eats too much.
B: A lot of patients don't really need treatment. They feel ill because they do
silly things. We can give them pills to treat some illnesses, but they need
to keep fit and eat sensibly.

4.2a **Listen, and repeat these things, which come from: a hospital,
a supermarket, a restaurant, a factory, a railway station.**

The machine in the corner needs cleaning.
Could you put clean sheets on Mrs Reed's bed, please?
Get the six fifteen train from platform three.
We need some more tinned peaches, and baked beans.
I'd like coffee with cream, and then the bill, please.

4.2b **Say which instruction came from which place.**

F U R T H E R P R A C T I C E

/ɪ/ Unit 1:1, 2, 4 pages 22–27

/æ/ hand   /e/ egg

TASK 1 Distinguish between /æ/ and /e/

1.1 Listen, and practise the difference.

had	head	mat	met
bag	beg	pack	peck
land	lend	marry	merry
can	Ken	pat	pet
pan	pen	cattle	kettle

**1.2 Listen to the words on the cassette.
Write the words you hear.**

**1.3 Listen to the sentences on the cassette.
For each one, write the word you hear.**

1 You have been using my pan/pen, haven't you?
2 He lost his bat/bet.
3 I can see a band/bend ahead.
4 We heard the cattle/kettle from a long way away.

TASK 2 Say /æ/

**2.1 Listen, and practise this telephone
conversation. Notice the telephonist's
polite, rising intonation.**

A: Cavendish Manufacturing Company. Can I help
you?

B: I'd like to speak to the Managing Director, please.

A: The Managing Director? That's Anna Cavendish.

I'll put you through.

2.2a Listen, and say the names on this noticeboard.

CAVENDISH MANUFACTURING COMPANY

Managing Director	Anna Cavendish
Marketing Manager	Barry Jackson
Development Manager	Andrew Maxwell
Architect	Pamela Andrews

**PW 2.2b Make telephone conversations like the one in
2.1, asking for different people each time.**

T A S K 3 Say /e/

3.1 Listen, and practise.

Only ten per cent of *Kensington Express* readers take regular exercise. In a recent survey, readers answered questions about diet and exercise. Ten per cent felt that they were healthy or very healthy. Seventy per cent said that exercise is important for good health. But only ten per cent took regular exercise – twice a week or more. Twenty per cent said that they felt they got enough exercise. The rest admitted that they should take more exercise.

3.2a Listen to people asking and answering questions. Notice the intonation. The voice rises in the questions, and falls in the answers.

Do you **feel** you are h**ea**lthy?

Y**e**s, I d**o**. I lead a v**e**ry healthy life.

Do you **think ex**ercise is im**por**tant for **good he**alth?

N**o**, I d**o**n't. Too much **ex**ercise can be d**a**ngerous.

3.2b Ask and answer the questions on this questionnaire.

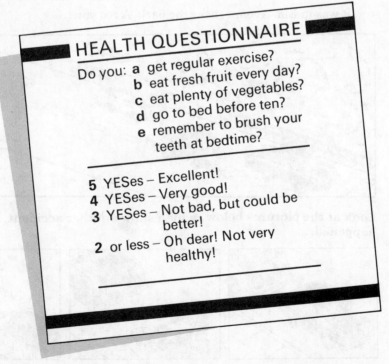

HEALTH QUESTIONNAIRE

Do you: a get regular exercise?
         b eat fresh fruit every day?
         c eat plenty of vegetables?
         d go to bed before ten?
         e remember to brush your
            teeth at bedtime?

5 YESes – Excellent!
4 YESes – Very good!
3 YESes – Not bad, but could be
          better!
2 or less – Oh dear! Not very
            healthy!

3.3 Discussion. What sort of exercise do people in the group take? What is regarded as healthy food in your community?

TASK 4   Say /æ/ and /e/

4a   **Listen, and practise this conversation about a car accident.**

A: I'm a reporter from the *Hendon Standard*. Were you present when the accident happened?
B: Yes, I was standing at the end of Elm Avenue, by the park.
A: What happened?
B: There was a red van travelling west, and several cars and vans behind it.
A: Was the red van going fast?
B: No. The driver kept glancing at a map on his lap. Then a black taxi started to pass the red van.
A: Was that the cause of the accident?
B: It wasn't the taxi that caused the accident. It was the red van. The van driver suddenly turned, and crashed into the taxi.
A: What happened then?
B: The taxi smashed into a lamppost. The taxi driver wasn't badly hurt, but he was very angry.

4b   **Look at the picture below, showing the scene of the accident described in 4a. Label the picture. Then say what happened.**

e.g. It was in Elm Avenue, near the park. A red van ....

4c   **Look at the pictures below, which show another accident. Say what happened.**

FURTHER PRACTICE
/æ/ Unit 25:1, 3, 4 page 97–99   /e/ Unit 1:1, 3, 4 page 22–27

TASK 1   Distinguish between /ʌ/ and /æ/

1.1   Listen, and practise the difference.

bug	bag	hut	hat
mud	mad	truck	track
puddle	paddle	much	match
fun	fan	drunk	drank
sung	sang	cup	cap
butter	batter	uncle	ankle

1.2   Listen to the words on the cassette.
Write the words you hear.

1.3   Listen to the sentences on the cassette.
For each one, write the word you hear.

1 I like my fish cooked in butter/batter.
2 He's worried about his uncle/ankle.
3 Put the rug/rag on the floor.
4 Here's a cup/cap for you.
5 I've lost the truck/track.
6 Does my hut/hat look nice?

TASK 2   Say /ʌ/

2a   Listen, and practise this conversation.

A: Uncle Cuthbert has just rung up.
B: Is he coming for lunch?
A: No, he's in trouble. There's been a flood.
B: But the flood was on Monday.
A: Now his truck is stuck in the mud.
B: He could come by bus.
A: No, the bus is stuck behind the truck. Nothing
 can move.

2b   Ask and answer. Try to use falling intonation on
these Wh-questions.

Who has **just rung up**?

Why can't Uncle Cuthbert **come** to **lunch**?

When was the **flood**?

Where is the **bus**?

SPELLING

/ʌ/ up

Common:
u (*short* **u**):
 cup, uncle,
 us, funny

Less common:
o   one, mother
ou   young,
     trouble
ough enough,
     rough
oo   blood, flood

Exception:
does

/æ/ hand

Common:
a (*short* **a**):
 sat, marry,
 hand, ran

Exception:
plait

TASK 3 Say /æ/

3a **Listen to six people saying what they did on Saturday.**

I swam the English Channel.
I got married.
I rang my grandmother.
I crashed my car.
I sang in a concert.
I sat at home.

3b **Look at the pictures. Say who did what.**

e.g. Ann Appleby got married.

1 Ann Appleby   2 Angela Lang   3 Harry Angus
4 Andrew Maxwell   5 Gavin Banks   6 Sally Paston

3c **The sentences below are incorrect. Listen, and repeat each one. Then say it with the correct facts.**

Sally Paston sang in a concert on Saturday.
Harry Angus got married on Saturday.
Ann Appleby sat at home on Saturday.
Gavin Banks swam the English Channel on Saturday.
Angela Lang crashed her car on Saturday.
Andrew Maxwell rang his grandmother on Saturday.

T A S K 4 Say /ʌ/ and /æ/

4.1 Listen, and say these phrases.

a Russian stamp	a black cupboard
a lovely hat	a flat cover
a sudden bang	an African hut
a dozen apples	a damp rug

4.2a Listen, and say what is on this menu.

LUNCHTIME
SNACKS

cup of tea
cup of coffee

ham sandwich
ham sandwich – with mustard
mixed salad
mixed salad – without onion

currant bun
jam sponge
apple pie and custard

bread and butter, with – plum jam
blackcurrant jam
honey

4.2b Listen, to someone saying what they would like. Notice the listing intonation.

e.g. 'I'd like a **cup** of **tea**, a **mixed sal**ad without **on**ion,

and some **bread** and **butter** with **plum jam**.'

Now choose, and say what you would like.

4.2c In a group, each person says what they would like. One person makes a list, then orders the food and drink for the whole group.

F U R T H E R   P R A C T I C E

/æ/ Unit 24:1, 2, 4 page 94, 96

/ɒ/ hot   /ɔː/ saw

TASK 1   Distinguish between /ɒ/ and /ɔː/

1.1   **Listen, and practise the difference.**

not	nought	spot	sport
stock	stalk	cod	cord
pot	port	cock	cork
cot	court	fox	forks

1.2   **Listen to the words on the cassette.
Write the words you hear.**

1.3   **Listen to the sentences on the cassette.
For each one, write the word you hear.**

1 They couldn't find the fox/forks
2 The pot/port was very old.
3 We saw the spot/sport.
4 The cod/cord isn't very good.
5 The cock/cork has been stolen.

TASK 2   Say /ɒ/

2a   **Listen, and say the things Johnny has to do.**

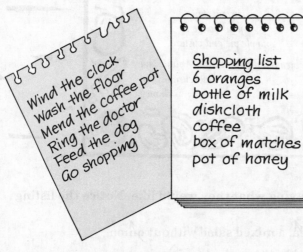

Wind the clock
Wash the floor
Mend the coffee pot
Ring the doctor
Feed the dog
Go shopping

Shopping list
6 oranges
bottle of milk
dishcloth
coffee
box of matches
pot of honey

SPELLING

/ɒ/ hot

Common:
ALL **o** + *final
consonant*:
     dog
ALL **ock** clock
ALL **o** + *double
consonant*:
     bottle

Less common:
a (*after* **w, wh,
     qu**):
     watch, what,
     quantity

Exceptions:
au because,
     sausage
ow knowledge

/ɔː/ saw

Common:
MOST **or**   horse
MOST **oar** board
ALL   **aw** saw,
            lawn
MOST **au**
            daughter

Less common:
a   all, water
ar (*after* **w, qu**):
     warm,
     quarter
oor door, floor
our four, court
ough + *consonant*:
     bought

GW **2b** Play the memory game. Each person chooses something from 2a, and remembers what other people said. Notice the listing intonation.

Example:

1ST PERSON: **John**ny has **got** to **buy** some **cof**fee.

2ND PERSON: **John**ny has **got** to **buy** some **cof**fee, and **wash** the **floor**.

3RD PERSON: **John**ny has **got** to **buy** some **cof**fee, **wash** the **floor**, and **wind** the **clock**.

4TH PERSON: ....

T A S K 3 Say /ɔː/

3.1 The past tense of these verbs contains the sound /ɔː/.

bring   buy   catch   fight   teach   think   wear

Listen, and say the past tenses.

3.2a Listen, and say these sentences.

The milkman brings four pints of milk every morning.
George buys a small Ford car every year.
Paul catches the ball.
My cat fights the dog next door.
Mr Morland teaches Law to forty-four students.
Gordon thinks Mr Morland's Law class is boring.
George wears a short-sleeved shirt.

3.2b Now change the sentences into the past.

e.g. Yesterday morning the milkman brought four pints of milk.

T A S K 4 Say /ɒ/ and /ɔː/

4.1 Listen, and say these phrases.

hot water	four o'clock
knock at the door	a tall bottle
stop talking	a small shop
a bottle of port	talk to the doctor

4.2   Listen, and practise this interview for a job.

A: Why do you want a job with the *Northern Record*?

B: I'd like to become a sports reporter. I always read the *Northern Record*. I saw your job advertisement. So I filled in an application form.

A: What other jobs have you done?

B: I've got a job in a sports shop, at the moment. Last August, I was a hotel porter. It was a holiday job, in a seaside resort.

A: Are you interested in sport?

B: Yes, I like watching football; I always watch my local football team when they play at the Sports Centre. I also watch sport on television quite often. And I go jogging every morning.

A: Right. Now, I'll tell you what this job involves .....

4.3   Listen, and practise this conversation.

A: Sorry to bother you, but I'm lost! I'm looking for the office of the local newspaper, the *Northern Record*.

B: It's opposite the Town Hall. Go along this road. At the crossroads, turn left. Then there's a department store called Potters. Opposite Potters, there's a small street. Walk up there, and you'll see the Town Hall on the right. The *Northern Record* office is opposite.

A: Is it a long way?

B: No, it's not far to walk.

A: Thank you very much.

B: Not at all.

4.4   Look at the map below. Ask and give directions, as in 4.3.

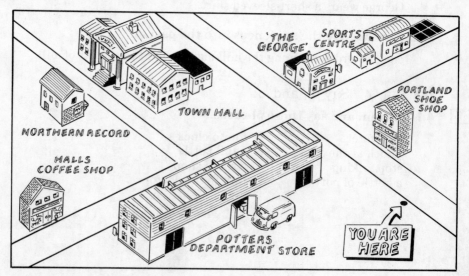

FURTHER PRACTICE

/ɔː/ Unit 27:1, 3, 4 pages 103–105

/əʊ/ home   /ɔː/ saw

TASK 1   Distinguish between /əʊ/ and /ɔː/

1.1 Listen, and practise the difference.

low	law	toe	tore
Joe	jaw	tone	torn
yoke, yolk	York	snow	snore
boat	bought	hole	hall
cold	called	sew, sow	saw
bowl	ball	show	shore

1.2 Listen to the words on the cassette. Write the words you hear.

law
jaw
York
boat
cold

1.3 Listen to the sentences on the cassette. For each one, write the word you hear.

1 The hole/hall is enormous.
2 I think your bowl/ball is in the kitchen.
3 The coal/call was delayed.
4 We're going to the show/shore next week.

TASK 2   Say /əʊ/

2.1a Listen to this airline pilot, and practise what he says.

Hello, this is Captain Oates speaking. Below us is the coast of Italy. We are very close to Rome – the road below us goes from Rome to the coast. We shall fly over the city before landing. Please obey the NO SMOKING notices.

2.1b Complete this extract from an airline magazine, and read it aloud.

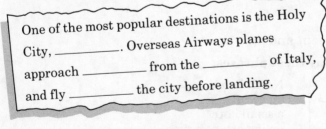

One of the most popular destinations is the Holy City, _____. Overseas Airways planes approach _____ from the _____ of Italy, and fly _____ the city before landing.

SPELLING

/əʊ/ home

Common:

ALL	**o**	*at the end of words:* so, ago
MOST	**o**	*with final* e: home, toe
SOME	**o**	*in the middle of words:* cold, both
MOST	**oa**	boat, coast

Less common:
ow low
ou shoulder

/ɔː/ saw

Common:

MOST	**or**	horse
MOST	**oar**	board
ALL	**aw**	saw, lawn
MOST	**au**	daughter

Less common:

a	all, water
ar (*after* **w, qu**):	warm, quarter
oor	door, floor
our	four, court
ough + *consonant*:	bought

2.2a Listen, and practise this conversation.

A: Could you go and post this letter, please?
B: I can't go out. It's snowing, and I've got a cold.
A: Blow your nose, and put your coat on. You'll be OK.
B: I'll get frozen.
A: Only if you go slowly. Walk quickly.
B: I can't walk quickly. The ground is frozen. It's like the South Pole.
A: Oh, stop moaning. I'll go.

2.2b Listen again to some of B's statements. He is making strong, definite statements, and his voice falls.

It's snowing.

I'll get frozen.

Now say the following statements, with a strong falling intonation.

I don't know where the post office is.
I've got a cold.
I haven't got a coat.
It's too cold.
The ground is frozen.

T A S K 3　Say /ɔ:/

Listen, and practise this conversation.

A: Hello, you're Gloria, aren't you? Mr Walker's small daughter?
B: Yes, I'm Gloria Walker. But I'm not small any more. I'm four and three-quarters.
A: Yes, you are quite tall, for four and three-quarters.
B: I'm taller than my friend Gordon, and he's five and a quarter.
A: Does Gordon live next door?
B: No. We live at number forty, and he lives at forty-four.

T A S K 4　Say /əʊ/ and /ɔ:/

4.1　Listen, and say these phrases.

roast pork	North Pole
an open door	an awful joke
a stone wall	a small hotel
a cold hall	an important notice

4.2a Listen to the conversations on the cassette. You will hear a hotel receptionist talking to guests. As you listen, tick the correct information on the forms below.

REGISTRATION FORM

NAME	Pauline Gordon/Paul O'Gordon
ADDRESS	4 Teencourt Road/14 Court Road
	Lower Wenlow/Lower Wenlaw
	Cornwall
ROOM	404/44

REGISTRATION FORM

NAME	Joe Norton/Joan Orton
ADDRESS	40 Newhole Street/14 Newhall Street
	Coldwater/Caldwater
	North Yorkshire
ROOM	14/40

4.2b Practise the conversations in 4.2a. Then copy the registration form. In pairs, make your own conversations; make up a name and address from the columns below. The receptionist should fill in the form during the conversation, repeating the information.

Gordon Golding	14	Holywell Lane	Coldwater	Cornwall
Gloria Rolls	4	Hall Road	Portland	North Yorkshire
Joan Walker	44	Lower Falls Road	Golders Green	London NW4
Joe Gordon	404	Court Road	Stonewater	West Yorkshire

FURTHER PRACTICE

/ɔː/ Unit 26:1, 3, 4 page 100–102

UNIT 28   /u:/ food   /ʊ/ put

T A S K 1   Distinguish between /u:/ and /ʊ/

1.1   Listen, and practise the difference.

fool	full	boot	foot
pool	pull	food	good
Luke	look	tool	wool

**1.2   Listen to the words on the cassette.
Write the words you hear.**

**1.3   Listen to these quotations*. Which sound is in
the words underlined – /u:/ or /ʊ/?**

A <u>good</u> <u>book</u> is the precious life blood of a master
spirit (*Milton*)

No sun – no <u>moon</u>!
No morn – no <u>noon</u>..... November! (*Hood*)

A <u>fool</u> and his money are <u>soon</u> parted. (*proverb*)

I <u>could</u> not love thee (Dear) so much,
Lov'd I not honour more. (*Lovelace*)

<u>Beauty</u> is <u>truth</u>, truth beauty. (*Keats*)

I like work ..... I can sit and <u>look</u> at it for hours.
(*Jerome K. Jerome*)

I was a stranger and you <u>took</u> me in. (*The Bible*)

* page 124 tells you where the quotations come from.

T A S K 2   Say /u:/

2.1a Listen, and say these places.

a supermarket   a shoe shop   a school
a chemist's   a café   a newsagent's
a tool shop

2.1b Listen, and say these sentences.

'Use a ruler.'
'I'd like some boots for the winter, and some shoes for
school.'
'Have you got any "Beauty-tooth" toothpaste?'
'Could I have some fruit juice?'
'A newspaper and some chewing gum, please.'
'Excuse me, where are the fruit and vegetables?'

SPELLING

/u:/ food

Common:
MANY **oo** food
        u ('*long
            u*')
            music
        u (*with
            final* **e**):
            June,
            blue
MOST **ew** chew

Less common:
o   do, move, shoe
ou soup, through
ui juice

Exception:
eau beautiful

/ʊ/ put

Common:
SOME **oo** good,
            book
        u put

Less common:
ou could
o   woman

2.1c Match each of the sentences in 2.1b with one of the places in 2.1a

e.g. 'Use a ruler' comes from a school.

T A S K 3 Say /ʊ/

3a Listen, and practise these conversations in a library. Notice how the librarian's voice rises; she repeats the customer's enquiry, while she thinks what to say.

A: Can I help you?

B: Yes, please. I'm looking for a book about woodwork.

A: A **book** about woodwork? What about *Woodwork for Beginners* by Peter Bull? It's full of good ideas.

B: Thank you. I'll look at it.

_____

A: Can I help you?

B: I hope so. I'm looking for a book about knitting.

A: A **book** about knitting? Here's a very good book called *Good Looking Woollens*, by Michael Foot. You could look at that.

B: Yes, that looks good.

3b Make similar conversations using the information given. The customer wants a book about the following.

knitting   wedding cakes   football (for a schoolboy)
the history of cooking

The librarian suggests one of these books.

Football Annual by the Football Association
Teach Yourself Football by Jack Woolmer
Pullovers for All by Catherine Hooker
Sugar Decoration for Cakes by Ann Pullen
Everywoman Guide to Craft and Cookery by Sally Booker
Cooks of the World by Kumud Patel

T A S K 4 Say /u:/ and /ʊ/

4.1 Listen, and say these phrases.

a foolish book	good food
a rude cook	a wooden spoon
blue wool	a full pool

4.2a Listen, and practise this extract from a radio programme.

JUDITH BROOKES: In the Food Programme studio today, we have two cooks, Julian Woolf and Susan Fuller. They are going to choose Christmas presents for a new cook. Julian Woolf, your kitchen is full of useful tools. If you could choose just two things for a new cook, what would you choose?

JULIAN WOOLF: I'd choose a fruit juice maker. You just put the fruit in and it produces fruit juice. It's super. And secondly, I'd choose a really good butcher's knife. Every cook could do with a good knife.

SUSAN FULLER: I'd choose a good cookery book, full of beautiful pictures. He could look at the book, and it would give him good ideas. And secondly, I'd choose a computer.

4.2b Listen to the next part of the conversation. Notice the interviewer's rising intonation on the question.

SUSAN FULLER: I'd choose a computer.

JUDITH BROOKES: A computer?

SUSAN FULLER: Yes, it would be useful, to keep a record of recipes and menus.

4.2c In groups, each person should choose something from the list below to give to a new cook. Think of a reason for your choice. Then make conversations like the one above.

a corkscrew   a big, blue, butcher's apron   a pudding basin
a wooden spoon   a soufflé dish   an ice cream scoop

4.3 Look at the recipe below. With a partner arrange the instructions in the correct order. Say the complete recipe. (Then you can listen to it on the cassette, to check.)

Julian Woolf's Winter Soup
Cut the roots into small cubes.
When it's cool, put the soup through a sieve.
Put them in a pan full of water.
You can make this soup with any root vegetables – potatoes, carrots, parsnips.
Cook them until they are soft.

TASK 1 Distinguish between /3:/ and /ɑ:/

1.1 Listen, and practise the difference.

firm	farm	dirt	dart
burn	barn	hurt	heart
stir	star	birth	bath
heard	hard	purse	pass

1.2 Listen to the words on the cassette.
Write the words you hear.

1.3 Listen to the sentences on the cassette.
For each one, write the word you hear.

1 He works for a firm/farm in the north.
2 I've lost my purse/pass.
3 The first/fast train leaves at seven o'clock.
4 She noticed the dirt/dart in the corner.

TASK 2 Say /3:/

2.1a Listen, and practise this conversation:

A: I'd like to reserve a seat on the ten thirty flight to Birmingham, on Thursday. My name is Vernon.
B: Thursday May 21st? Certainly, sir. There's a seat in the third row.
A: That's fine. And I'm returning on May 23rd.
B: The first flight leaves Birmingham at eight thirty.
A: That's a bit early.
B: Or there's twelve thirty, or four thirty.
A: Four thirty's too late. Twelve thirty, please.
B: On the twelve thirty flight on May 23rd, there's only a seat free in row thirteen.
A: Row thirteen*? No, thanks. I'll go at eight thirty.

* Some people believe 13 is an unlucky number.

SPELLING

/3:/ bird

Common:
ALL **er, ir, ur**
+ *consonant or stressed at the end of words*:
her, verb, prefer, fir, girl, first, fur, turn, church

Less common:
w + **or** word, work
our journey, courtesy
ear learn, earth

/ɑ:/ car

Common:
MOST **ar** artist, car, park
SOME **a** father, half

Less common:
ear heart
er sergeant, clerk
au aunt, laugh

(PW) **2.1b** **Ask and answer questions. Try to use a falling intonation on these**
** **   **Wh-questions.**

Where is Mr Vernon go↘ing?

When is he tr↘avelling?

Which row is his se↘at in?

What date is he ret↘urning?

What t↘ime?

Why doesn't he **want** a seat on the **twelve-thi↘rty flight?**

2.2 **Listen, and practise this conversation between a driving instructor**
     and a learner driver.

A: Take the third turning on the right. Then stop by the church. I'd like you
   to reverse round that corner.
B: Yes, I certainly need to practise reversing.
   (*stops and reverses*)
A: Not bad. But you weren't close enough to the kerb. Turn the steering
   wheel further to the left.
B: OK. Last lesson I turned it too much, and I was too close to the kerb.
   (*tries again*) Oh dear, that was worse.
A: We'll return to reversing later. Now drive on. Turn right by the big fir
   tree.
B: I need to learn how to do an emergency stop.
A: Yes, when we've gone a bit further. Take the first turning – mind that
   little girl! Well done, that was a perfect emergency stop.

T A S K 3 Say /ɑː/

Listen, and read out this newspaper advertisement.

■BARKERS DEPARTMENT STORE■

―――― Marvellous bargains! ――――

CARPETS – half price
CHRISTMAS CARDS – large and small
OXFORD MARMALADE – 30p a jar
GARDEN CHAIRS – with and without arms
CARDBOARD PLATES – ideal for parties
ARTISTS' MATERIALS
TOY FARM – includes farmhouse, barn and animals

TASK 4 Say /ɜ:/ and /ɑ:/

4.1 Listen, and read out this newspaper advertisement.

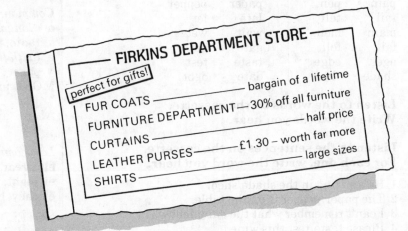

4.2a Listen, and repeat these sentences.

Margaret Irwin is moving into a new flat soon.
Martha Kirby is going on holiday to Siberia.
Marcus Irving is having a party at the weekend.
Shirley Parkes is a commercial artist.
Carl Parker's son is five next week.
John Darling is tall and fat.

4.2b Look at the articles advertised in the sales at Barkers and Firkins
Department Stores in 3 and 4.1. Discuss which articles would be
suitable for each of the people above.

e.g. Margaret Irwin could buy furniture for her new flat, at Firkins.

4.3a Listen to a news story about an accident.

4.3b The sentences below come from the news story in 4.3a.
Put them in the right order, and practise telling the story.

6 His father drove him to the hospital Emergency Department.
3 Bernard had some fireworks.
7 A nurse cleaned the dirt off the burn.
1 Bernard Parker, aged thirteen, had a birthday party yesterday.
5 He was badly hurt.
2 But the party turned into a tragedy.
4 The very first firework went off in Bernard's face.
8 Then he was transferred to the Burns Unit, for surgery.

T A S K 1 Distinguish between /eɪ/ and /e/

1.1 Listen, and practise the difference.

pain	pen	paper	pepper
tail	tell	late	let
main	men	wait	wet
fail	fell	gate	get
age	edge	taste	test
shade	shed	date	debt

1.2 Listen to the words on the cassette.
Write the words you hear.

1.3 Listen to the sentences on the cassette.
For each one, write the word you hear.

1 He's sitting in the shade/shed.
2 The paper/pepper is on the table.
3 I can't remember what the date/debt was.
4 Please taste/test this wine.
5 They're sailing/selling their boat next week.

T A S K 2 Say /eɪ/

2.1a Listen, and read out the names of these people
coming for an interview.

memo

Interview Times

8·30 James Gray   11·00 Phillip Lane

9·00 John Day   11·30 Kay Waite

9·30 Graham Lay   12·00 Tracey Capes

10·00 May Frazer   12·30 Kate Mace

10·30 Jane Hayes

2.1b Listen to someone correcting mistakes. Notice how the voice falls and
rises on the incorrect information, then falls to emphasise the correct
information.

A: 8.30, John Day.

B: **No**, the **person** at **8.30** isn't **John Day**. It's **James Gray**.

A: 10.00, Jay Frazer

B: **No**, it isn't **Jay Frazer**, it's **May Frazer**.

2.1c Below are some more mistakes. Correct them, using the information
in the list in 2.1a.

9.30 Kay Waite

10.00 Jane Hayes

12.00 Phillip Lane

10.00 Kay Frazer

11.30 Jane Waite

12.30 James Mace

2.1d Make some more mistakes about the times or names in 2.1a. Your
partner must correct the mistakes.

2.2a Listen, and practise this conversation at a newsagent's.

CUSTOMER: Hello. My name is Jameson. I live at 28 Daisy Way. We have
our newspapers delivered.

NEWSAGENT: Yes sir. How can I help you?

CUSTOMER: This week, the papers have been late every day. And on
Wednesday, we didn't get any papers at all.

NEWSAGENT: Which papers do you have?

CUSTOMER: *The Daily Telegraph* and the *Daily Mail*.

NEWSAGENT: Oh yes. I can explain. The *Daily Mail* came late. There was a
breakdown at the printers. And *The Daily Telegraph* is on
strike.

CUSTOMER: That's very strange. Well, can I take the *Daily Mail* now?

NEWSAGENT: I'm afraid we're still waiting for it.

CUSTOMER: Will you send it, when it arrives?

NEWSAGENT: Yes, I'll send it straight away.

[cassette icon] **2.2b Listen, and practise the intonation of these alternative questions.**

Is the customer's name James or Jameson?

Does he live in Daisy Way or Daisy Lane?

Is the problem about magazines or newspapers?

He didn't get any newspapers one day. Was it Wednesday or Thursday?

Does he have *The Daily Telegraph* or *The Times*?

Does he have the *Daily Express* or the *Daily Mail*?

[cassette icon] **2.2c Ask and answer the questions using the information in 2.2a.**

[PW icon]

e.g. A: Is the **customer's name James** or **Jameson**?

B: His **name's Jameson**.

T A S K 3   Say /eɪ/ and /e/

[cassette icon] **3a Listen, and practise these conversations at an airport information desk.**

A: Excuse me, I'm waiting for
someone from Spain.
Which plane is it?
B: Flight BA 287.
A: When is it due?
B: 8.28.
A: Is it on time?
B: No, I'm afraid it's late.

C: Excuse me, I'm waiting for someone
from Belgium. Which plane is it?
B: Flight BA 280.
C: When is it due?
B: 8.10.
C: Is it on time?
B: Yes, it is.

3b Make similar conversations, using information from the airport arrivals information board.

ARRIVALS			
FLIGHT NO	FROM	TIME DUE	
BA 280	Belgium	8.10	on time
BA 282	Edinburgh	8.17	delayed
BA 286	Denmark	8.25	on time
BA 287	Spain	8.28	delayed
BA 289	Norway	8.38	delayed

F U R T H E R P R A C T I C E

/e/ Unit 1:3, 4 page 24–27;   Unit 24:3, 4 page 95–96

TASK 1   Distinguish between /eə/ and /ɪə/

1.1   Listen, and practise the difference.

hair	here, hear	dare	dear, deer
bear	beer	chair	cheer
air	ear	Clare	clear
fair, fare	fear	stare	steer
rare	rear	spare	spear
pear	pier	rarely	really

**1.2   Listen to the words on the cassette.
Write the words you hear.**

**1.3   Listen to the sentences on the cassette.
For each one, write the word you hear.**

1 They gave her three chairs/cheers.
2 The bear/beer was awful.
3 The pear/pier is rotten.
4 He is rarely/really unhappy.
5 The driver of that car is staring/steering at us.

TASK 2   Say /eə/

**2.1   Listen, and practise the conversation.
Listen carefully to the intonation.**

A: Excuse me, I'm looking for Miss O'Dare. Do you
know where she is?

B: She's gone to Trafalgar Square.

A: Do you know where, exactly?

B: To the Headquarters of the Dairy Council.

A: Why has she gone there?

B: She has got a dairy. It's called Mary's Dairy.

A: I thought she was a hairdresser.

B: Oh you mean Clare O'Dare. She's upstairs. It's her
sister Mary who's gone to Trafalgar Square.

2.2a Listen, and say these names of shops.

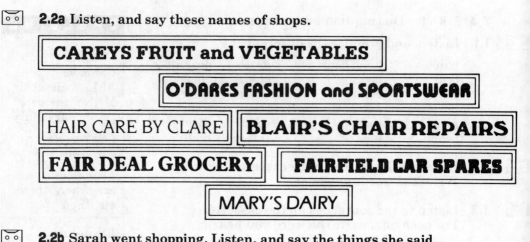

CAREYS FRUIT and VEGETABLES

O'DARES FASHION and SPORTSWEAR

HAIR CARE BY CLARE   BLAIR'S CHAIR REPAIRS

FAIR DEAL GROCERY   FAIRFIELD CAR SPARES

MARY'S DAIRY

2.2b Sarah went shopping. Listen, and say the things she said.

'I'd like some pears.'   'Where's the milk, please?'
'Could I have my hair cut?'   'This chair's broken.'
'Is there any oil?'   'I need a new spare tyre.'
'Oh, I couldn't wear that!'

2.2c Match the things Sarah said with the shops in 2.2a.

e.g. She said 'I'd like some pears' in Carey's Fruit and Vegetables.

T A S K 3   Say /ɪə/

3a   Listen, and read out this letter.

LEARY BEER COMPANY
'Brewers of real beer for 70 years'
21 Clearwater Avenue,
Bere Regis

Mr A. J. Pierce,
Pierce's Detective Agency,
14 Steerforth Street,
Bere Regis

Dear Mr Pierce,

We have a serious problem here at Leary's. Barrels of beer keep disappearing
from the cellar. I fear we have a thief here. It is clear to me that your
experience would be valuable in solving these mysterious disappearances.

Yours sincerely,

R.G.Leary.

P. G. Leary

3b **Use information from the letter in 3a to complete the conversation below. Practise the conversation.**

MR PIERCE: Pierce's Detective Agency. Can I help you?

MR LEARY: Good morning. My name is _____,

from the _____ _____ Company.

I fear we have a _____ problem.

MR PIERCE: Oh dear. What appears to be happening?

MR LEARY: Barrels of _____ are _____ from the

cellar.

MR PIERCE: Has beer ever disappeared before?

MR LEARY: No. The Leary Beer Company has been brewing

_____ for _____

_____, and no beer has ever _____

before this _____. It appears that we have a thief

_____. It is clear that we need someone with your

_____ to solve these _____

_____.

T A S K 4 Say /eə/ and /ɪə/

4a **Listen, and practise the conversation.**

A: I've brought my car in for repair.
B: OK, leave it here, and we'll take care of it. What's the trouble?
A: There are various things. Some are serious, some not so serious. The gear box is really bad. It won't go into top gear.
B: Yes, that does sound serious.
A: The steering wheel is stiff. And the radio aerial doesn't work.
B: You may need a new aerial. They wear out quickly.
A: But it's only three years old.
B: You can't get spare parts. So if one part wears out, you have to have a new aerial.
A: I see. And would you repair the spare wheel? The air comes out.

4b **Listen and notice the falling intonation of these Wh-questions. Then ask and answer the questions.**

Which four things in the **car** need rep**air**ing?

What is the **problem** with **each thing**?

Which do you **think** is **most serious**?

Which is le**ast serious**?

/aɪ/ five /ɔɪ/ boy
/aʊ/ now

TASK 1 Say /aɪ/

1.1a Listen, and say these words.
Notice which words contain /aɪ/.

List A: (white) kitchen pint ripe apple
ice sharp fried

List B: pie glass knife cream table
(wine) rice fruit

1.1b Put a word from List A with a word from List B
to make a phrase connected with cooking,
eating or drinking.

e.g. white wine

1.2a Listen, and say these sums:

$5 \times 5 = 25$ Five times five makes twenty-five.
$9 \div 3 = 3$ Nine divided by three makes three.
$90 - 5 = 85$ Ninety minus five makes eighty-five.

1.2b Say these sums, with the answers!

$5 \times 9 =$	$99 \div 9 =$
$35 \div 5 =$	$19 - 5 =$
$19 - 10 =$	$9 \times 10 =$

TASK 2 Say /ɔɪ/

2.1 Listen, and practise this conversation:

A: Could I make an appointment with Doctor Boyle?
B: I'm afraid all Dr Boyle's appointments are taken today.
A: How annoying! I like Dr Boyle.
B: Sorry to disappoint you. Now, you've got a choice. You could make an appointment to see Dr Boyle tomorrow, or see Dr Lloyd today.
A: My employer has given me time off to go to the doctor. I'd better see Dr Lloyd today.

SPELLING

/aɪ/ five

Common:
i (*'long i'*):
blind, sign,
island, pint
i (*with final* e):
write, five,
die, arrive
y (*stressed*):
apply, try, dye
igh high, light

Exceptions:
eye
ei either,
neither
uy buy, guy

/ɔɪ/ boy

ALL **oi** boil,
rejoice
ALL **oy** toy,
enjoy

NOTE:
oi *comes at the beginning and in the middle of words. At the end of words the spelling is* **oy**.

/aʊ/ now

MANY **ou** house,
out,
ground
MANY **ow** brown,
how,
towel

2.2a Listen, and repeat these sentences with question tags. The speaker is certain, and expects the other person to agree.

Doctor Boyle is very good, isn't he?

Most people want to see Doctor Boyle, don't they?

All his appointments are taken, aren't they?

2.2b Say the following sentences, adding a question tag.

It's annoying,
A is disappointed,
You could see Dr Boyle tomorrow,
You could see Dr Lloyd today,
A is going to make an appointment with Dr Lloyd today,

2.3 Look at the recipe below. With a partner, arrange the instructions in the correct order. Say the complete recipe. (Then you can listen to it on the cassette, to check.)

Baked Potatoes
Wrap in foil to keep moist.
Boil for 20 minutes.
Scrub to remove soil.
Brush each potato with a little oil.
Bake in a hot oven for 40 minutes.
Remove from boiling water and drain.

TASK 3 Say /aʊ/

Listen, and read out three extracts from hotel brochures.

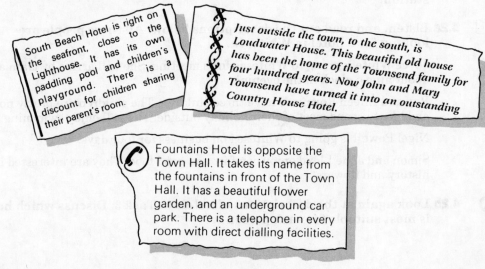

South Beach Hotel is right on the seafront, close to the Lighthouse. It has its own paddling pool and children's playground. There is a discount for children sharing their parent's room.

Just outside the town, to the south, is Loudwater House. This beautiful old house has been the home of the Townsend family for four hundred years. Now John and Mary Townsend have turned it into an outstanding Country House Hotel.

Fountains Hotel is opposite the Town Hall. It takes its name from the fountains in front of the Town Hall. It has a beautiful flower garden, and an underground car park. There is a telephone in every room with direct dialling facilities.

T A S K 4 Say /aɪ/ and /ɔɪ/ and /aʊ/

4.1a Look at the map of Whitesea, below. With a partner, identify the three hotels described in Task 3.

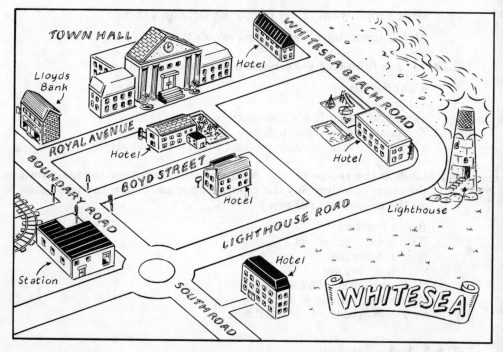

4.1b Look at the map. For each of the hotels, give directions from the station.

4.2a Listen, and read out the descriptions below. All these people are looking for a hotel in Whitesea.

Joyce White is going to Whitesea for a meeting. She will arrive by train at about nine o'clock in the evening.

Roy and Eileen Rowntree have three children. The children are pretty noisy, and like to spend most of their holiday outside. They all enjoy swimming.

Nigel Powell is going to Whitesea on business for four days.

Simon and Jane Lloyd enjoy comfort and good food. They are interested in history and flowers.

4.2b Look again at the descriptions of hotels in Task 3. Discuss which hotel is most suitable for each person.

Key

UNIT 1 INTRODUCTORY UNIT
1.2 1 peg 2 hid 3 fill 4 medal 5 cheque 6 miss 7 pet 8 left 9 sit
      10 lid 11 head 12 mess
1.3 1 bell 2 pen 3 tin 4 chick 5 lead 6 will

UNIT 2
1.2 1 see 2 sell 3 shed 4 save 5 mesh 6 parish 7 ass 8 fist 9 shock
      10 saw 11 show 12 Sue 13 sort 14 push 15 rushed 16 crust
1.3 1 socks 2 shack 3 seat 4 sifting 5 ship 6 shine

UNIT 3
1.2 1 ship 2 sherry 3 choose 4 cheap 5 share 6 shops 7 watching
      8 cash 9 match 10 wish 11 crutch 12 ditches
1.3 1 chops 2 dishes 3 match 4 washing

UNIT 4
1.2 1 gin 2 cheer 3 joke 4 Jane 5 rich 6 search 7 age 8 larch
      9 chin 10 ridge
1.3 1 joking 2 cheered 3 large 4 chin
2b aren't you? weren't you? don't you?

UNIT 5
1.2 1 yet 2 use 3 Jack 4 yeti 5 yam 6 yolk, yoke 7 jeer 8 Jess
      9 yet 10 juice 11 Jack 12 jam
1.3 1 jam 2 yolks 3 years 4 jetty
3.2a 6 January – Christian Feast of Epiphany; 4 July – Independence Day, USA;
      14 July – Bastille Day, France; 1 January – New Year's Day; 21 June –
      longest day of the year
3.3 1 jam 2 juice 3 gin 4 cabbage 5 ginger 6 orange

UNIT 6
1.2 1 Sue 2 said 3 zeal 4 lacy 5 fuzzy 6 zip 7 rise 8 loose 9 raise
      10. advice 11 ones 12 lice
1.3 1 peace 2 prize 3 lies 4 sip 5 buzz 6 pence
3.2 razor   rise   eyes   Caesar   lazy   freeze   seize   crazy
      easy

UNIT 7
1.2 1 hand 2 all 3 ear 4 high 5 eight 6 art 7 harm 8 ill 9 his
      10 old 11 hat 12 air
1.3 1 heart 2 hair 3 edge 4 eat
3.2b 1 keyhole 2 greenhouse 3 unusual 4 react 5 alcohol 6 workout
      7 unhurt 8 rehearse
3.4b Anton Hardy got something in his ear.
      Harriet Adler was hit in the eye by a hammer.
      Ann Herring hurt her ankle on her husband's umbrella.
      Andrew Hall fell off a horse.

UNIT 8
1.2 1 pit   2 bat   3 port   4 bull   5 pride   6 rope   7 tribe   8 tap   9 cub
      10 rib
1.3 1 pet   2 pin   3 bears   4 peach   5 blaze   6 robe   7 tripe   8 rib

UNIT 9
1.2 1 do   2 den   3 ton   4 town   5 drain   6 side   7 heart   8 plate   9 bad
      10 set
1.3 1 trains   2 dyed   3 trunk   4 rides   5 cart   6 hit   7 bed
3b   David **phoned**. His **shoulder** is **bad**. He's **gone** to the **doctor's**.
      Duncan **Dud**ley's **dep**uty **phoned**. **Dun**can is on **hol**iday in **Devon**.
      He will be **there** from **Mon**day to **Fri**day.

UNIT 10
1.2 1 could   2 cot   3 goat   4 cave   5 glue   6 league   7 pick   8 log
      9 angle   10 crow
1.3 1 cards   2 girl   3 cold   4 class   5 clue   6 bag   7 log

UNIT 11
1.2 1 rip   2 lap   3 right   4 law   5 read   6 wrist   7 berry   8 collect
      9 alive   10 long   11 rap, wrap   12 law
1.3 1 lead   2 list   3 right   4 collecting   5 wrong   6 Lyon
2.2b Who does the castle belong to?   Where do the Lumley family live?
      Who lives in the castle?   Where are we going?   What time is it?
4.2b doesn't she? isn't it? isn't it? isn't it? isn't it? haven't they?

UNIT 12
1.2 1 low   2 night   3 net   4 Lee   5 lip   6 knife   7 Kenny   8 collect   9 no
      10 let
1.3 1 no   2 life   3 night   4 Kelly   5 connected

UNIT 13
1.2 1 van   2 very   3 fail   4 veal   5 fine   6 foal   7 leaf   8 save   9 a life
      10 believe   11 prove
1.3 1 vole   2 fan   3 few   4 fines   5 vast
1.5 1 faint   2 pale   3 fast   4 foot   5 pray   6 pair, pear   7 fit   8 palm
      9 feel   10 pat   11 coffee   12 fort
1.6 1 full   2 fair   3 pigs   4 peas   5 fan   6 port
5.1 1 A dolphin is not a fish; it is a mammal.
      2 Potatoes are not fruit; they are vegetables.
      3 Penguins cannot fly.
      4 Tigers don't come from Africa, they come from India.
      5 The country which produces most coffee is Brazil.
      6 The first people to fly the Atlantic were Alcock and Brown in 1919.
6   **Tapescript**
      Please put the frozen vegetables in the freezer, the peas at the front. Then
      put the fresh fruit and vegetables on the shelves next to the freezer – the
      vegetables on the right. The potatoes are in four-pound bags. Put those on
      the floor. And be careful. They are very heavy. Lift them one at a time.

Then put the other vegetables on the shelves above. Fruit goes on the shelves on the left of the freezer. Fill the bottom shelf first, with apples and pears. Then put the peaches and the other fresh fruit on the next shelf. And the dried fruit on the top shelf – first the apricots, on the left, then the figs and finally the prunes.

Key
1 apricots 2 figs 3 prunes 4 peaches and other fruit 5 apples and pears
6 frozen vegetables 7 peas 8 vegetables 9 vegetables 10 potatoes

UNIT 14
1.2 1 best 2 boat 3 vole 4 bat 5 very 6 bolts 7 ban 8 vet 9 vest
10 vote
1.3 1 boat 2 vole 3 bolts 4 ban 5 vet
1.5 1 wet 2 vest 3 wail, whale 4 verse 5 via 6 vine 7 we 8 wheel
1.6 1 wheel 2 west 3 vines 4 whales 5 verse
4 What did he hear? When did he hear something wonderful?
What time did she go to work? What did she have?
Why did she go out through the window? (*etc.*)

UNIT 15
1.2 1 sin 2 rang 3 ton 4 sun 5 singer 6 wing 7 thin 8 bang 9 win
10 sinner
1.3 1 sinning 2 rang 3 ban 4 singer

UNIT 16
1.2 1 thick 2 sink 3 theme 4 sum 5 sing 6 path 7 mouth 8 moss
9 worth 10 tense
1.3 1 thinking 2 thumb 3 pass 4 mouse 5 moth
1.5 1 breathe 2 teasing 3 closing 4 bathe 5 Zen 6 breathing 7 then
8 teethe 9 bays 10 clothed
5.2 1 finger 2 North Pole 3 throw it 4 3rd month 5 unhealthy
5.2c 1 certain 2 certain 3 not certain 4 certain 5 not certain 6 certain
7 not certain 8 certain 9 certain
5.3 isn't it? wasn't it? isn't it? hasn't she? isn't it? isn't he? isn't she?
doesn't she? don't they?

UNIT 17
1.2 1 tin 2 thank 3 tick 4 three 5 theme 6 heath 7 sheet 8 fourth
9 part 10 nought 11 thick 12 heath
1.3 1 thought 2 team 3 tin 4 path 5 heath
1.5 1 dare 2 then 3 Dan 4 though 5 breed 6 worthy 7 ladder
8 breathing 9 dare 10 than
5.2a Tapescript
My name is Judith Smith. I am the oldest in my family. I've got two sisters and one brother. I'm nineteen now, and my sister Catherine is sixteen. There is three years between us, and there is also three years between Catherine and my other sister, Ruth. Then there's Jonathan, who's eight. My mother and father are both thirty-nine. Their names are Elizabeth and Arthur.

Key
The Smith Family. Elizabeth & Arthur both 39, Judith 19, Catherine 16, Ruth 13, Jonathan 8

UNIT 18

1.2   1 free   2 thirst   3 thread   4 frill   5 half   6 Ruth   7 death   8 four
9 Fred   10 half   11 three
1.3   1 fin   2 thaw   3 fought   4 three

UNIT 19

2.2   1 school   2 skate   3 ski   4 snow   5 sleep   6 slice   7 Scotland

UNIT 23

1.2   1 green   2 bead   3 risen   4 mill   5 fit   6 cheek   7 deep   8 itch
9 risen   10 feet
1.3   1 beans   2 live   3 fill   4 peach   5 bit   6 beaten

UNIT 24

1.2   1 had   2 beg   3 lend   4 can   5 pan   6 met   7 peck   8 marry   9 pat
10 kettle   11 head   12 pack
1.3   1 pen   2 bat   3 bend   4 cattle

UNIT 25

1.2   1 bug   2 mud   3 puddle   4 fan   5 sang   6 batter   7 hut   8 track
9 match   10 drunk   11 cap   12 uncle
1.3   1 butter   2 ankle   3 rag   4 cup   5 track   6 hat

UNIT 26

1.2   1 not   2 stalk   3 pot   4 court   5 sport   6 cod   7 cork   8 fox   9 sport
10 port
1.3   1 forks   2 pot   3 spot   4 cord   5 cock

UNIT 27

1.2   1 law   2 jaw   3 yoke, yolk   4 bought   5 cold   6 bowl   7 toe   8 torn
9 snow   10 hole   11 saw   12 shore
1.3   1 hole   2 ball   3 call   4 show
4.2a   NAME: Pauline Gordon   NAME: Joe Norton
ADDRESS: 14 Court Road   ADDRESS: 40 Newhole Street
           Lower Wenlaw   Coldwater
           Cornwall   North Yorkshire
ROOM: 404   ROOM: 40

UNIT 28

1.2   1 full   2 pull   3 look   4 fool   5 pull   6 Luke
1.3   /uː/ moon, noon, fool, soon, truth, beauty
         /ʊ/ good, book, could, look, took

References:
John Milton   *Areopagitica*
Thomas Hood   *November*
Richard Lovelace *To Lucasta, Going to the Wars*
John Keats   *Ode on a Grecian Urn*
Jerome K. Jerome   *Three Men in a Boat*, Chap. 15
The Bible *St Matthew*, Chap. 25, verse 35

UNIT 29
1.2 1 firm 2 barn 3 star 4 heard 5 dart 6 hurt 7 bath 8 purse
   9 barn 10 dirt
1.3 1 farm 2 purse 3 fast 4 dirt

UNIT 30
1.2 1 pen 2 tail 3 main 4 fail 5 edge 6 shade 7 pepper 8 late
   9 wet 10 get 11 taste 12 date
1.3 1 shed 2 paper 3 debt 4 test 5 sailing

UNIT 31
1.2 1 here, hear 2 beer 3 air 4 fair, fare 5 rear 6 pear 7 dare
   8 cheer 9 Clare 10 stare 11 spare 12 really
1.3 1 cheers 2 bear 3 pier 4 rarely 5 steering

UNIT 32
1.2b Five times nine makes forty-five.
   Thirty-five divided by five makes seven.
   Nineteen minus ten makes nine.
   Ninety-nine divided by nine makes eleven.
   Nineteen minus five makes fourteen.
   Nine times ten makes ninety.
2.2b isn't it? isn't he/she? couldn't you? couldn't you? isn't he/she?